# What Readers are Saying

Building upon years of experience in coaching congregations, Kay and Ken brought the map, a practical step-by-step guidebook for retreat facilitators, pastors, and church leaders to prayerfully discern a strategy to make disciples of Jesus Christ. They provide all the tools for a leadership team's strategic planning retreat, from recruiting the "right" group and assigning pre-work, through implementation, and even providing follow-up accountability. Don't get lost in the weeds of strategic planning. Let *Strategy Matters: Your Roadmap for an Effective Ministry Planning Retreat* be your map for navigating your next planning retreat.

**Blake Bradford**
Arkansas Conference of The UMC

A concise, practical primer for leading effective strategic planning retreats, *Strategy Matters* outlines all aspects of leading a retreat from preparing the participants ahead of time and conducting the retreat, to helpful follow-through. I wish I had this helpful resource 20 years ago.

**Dirk Elliott**
Director of Congregational Vibrancy, Michigan Conference of The UMC

I love *Strategy Matters: A Road Map for an Effective Planning Retreat.* Kotan & Willard have collected wisdom, resources, and ideas in one convenient resource. Anyone from a novice to the most seasoned retreat facilitator will find nuggets of insight in this gem.

**Jaye Johnson**
Director of Congregational Excellence, Iowa Conference of The UMC

Order copies of Ken's books from:
https://ken-willard-pcc.square.site/

In this fast paced and ever-changing world, a world that tempts the church and its leaders to lose focus, a values-based discernment and planning process has never been more important. Ken and Kay challenge leaders to intentionally and prayerfully look to see where God is already active in their communities and life. Building upon that discovery, they then present a practical and strategic guidance process to help the Church determine how the faith community can join God's work and make the difference God is calling them to make. Their book is a practical and spiritual guidance process that helps congregations and leadership to move in strategic, life-giving ways.

**Bishop Sandra Steiner Ball**
Resident Bishop West Virginia Conference of The UMC

# Acknowledgments

It has been my privilege to work in both the secular world as a banker and owner of three businesses as well as work in ministry as a local church leader, coach, consultant, and conference director. In each of these roles, strategic planning has been a significant part of the work. Each unique setting brought its particular nuances. Yet, there is a consistent underlying foundation of the basic theory of strategic planning and its importance to the organizational health and vitality. I am so appreciative of each of these seasons and roles. They have helped continuously inform my work in walking alongside so many churches over this past decade. Thank you to all the pastors, laity leaders, and churches across the country who have graciously allowed me to walk alongside them over the years. Each of those experiences inform the future work where others will continuously benefit.

To my friend, colleague, and mentor, Ken Willard. I will forever be in your debt for what you have taught me and all the experiences over the years as you have walked alongside me in ministry.

To the two favorite men in my life, my husband Bob and my son Cameron. I am beyond words to express my gratitude for your unwavering support and encouragement in this past decade of ministry. You have seen me through the highest of highs and the lowest of lows. You have both been my biggest cheerleaders even in times when it has meant sacrifice for you personally. I am eternally grateful and my heart overflows.

**Kay**

*Continued on following page*

I spent many years doing various types of strategic planning in the business world. Everything from teaching courses on setting goals to helping organizations identify and live into their core values. Little did I know that during that time God was preparing me to do strategic ministry planning with churches. It has been such a joy to work with pastors and churches all over the country as we partner together into God's future for their ministry. Many people have helped me along the way to transfer and adapt concepts into the church world. Leaders such as my friend Rev. Mike Schreiner at Morning Star Church; Dr. Aubrey Malphurs who authored the wonderful book, *Advanced Strategic Planning: A New Model for Church and Ministry Leaders;* Jim Barber the President of the Society for Church Consulting who trained and equipped me to work with churches; Bishop Sandra Steiner Ball and Rev. Dr. Bonnie MacDonald with whom I have the pleasure and joy to be in ministry; and Rev. Dr. David Hyatt and Kay Kotan who I have been very blessed to call friends and partners on this journey.

As always, my wife Mary, who is my rock and my inspiration. Thanks for putting up with me.

**Ken**

KAY KOTAN & KEN WILLARD

# STRATEGY MATTERS

### YOUR ROADMAP FOR AN EFFECTIVE MINISTRY PLANNING RETREAT

**Foreword by Rev. Lisa Greenwood**

Market
Square
BOOKS

# Strategy Matters

*Your Roadmap for an Effective Ministry Planning Retreat*

©2020 Kay Kotan & Ken Willard

books@marketsquarebooks.com
P.O. Box 23664  Knoxville, Tennessee 37933

ISBN: 978-1-950899-12-8
Library of Congress: 2020936460

Printed and Bound in the United States of America
Cover Illustration & Book Design ©2019 Market Square Publishing, LLC

Publisher: Kevin Slimp
Editor: Kristin Lighter
Post-Process Editor: Ken Rochelle

## Scripture quotations taken from the following versions of the Holy Bible as noted:

# Table of Contents

# Foreword

It's clear the days of 10-or 20-year, long range planning are over. Our rapidly changing times demand a high level of adaptability and flexibility as we seek to live into our mission of making disciples. Kay Kotan and Ken Willard remind us in this very practical field guide that while a 15-year plan might be a thing of the past, it is more important than ever to invest in intentional, strategic ministry planning.

In our work with churches through the Texas Methodist Foundation, we have noticed that many church leaders confuse discernment with planning and outcomes with activities. Both are necessary, but they are not the same thing. Planning without discernment may keep you busy, but is not likely to help you make the difference God is calling you to make. Activities that are not focused on defined outcomes are a drain on resources, and are more likely to lead to exhaustion rather than to effectiveness.

When Kay and Ken encourage church leaders to engage in annual strategic planning retreats, they are pointing the church toward something much deeper than planning activities. They are challenging leaders to take time to pay attention to what God is doing and saying in their community and in their own lives, so the Church can focus on the difference God is calling them to make.

In reading this guide, I am struck by a couple of observations. First, if you truly follow their wisdom, you'll find that the work is more than a two-day retreat. It involves weeks, even months, of preparation. Their process invites you into faithful discernment that includes listening, paying attention, having conversations, making observations, and praying. The process is most fruitful when the leaders invest in the entire process, owning the importance of every step along the way, from understanding the mission field to listening for God's leading.

The other observation is that we may be tempted to make this process linear: first you discern, then you plan. The truth is the process is more layered than linear. You'll notice that throughout each step, Kay and Ken consistently call the leaders back to prayer. Prayer is a layer that permeates the whole process. Listening is another layer throughout the process—listening to the nudging of the Holy Spirit, listening to your neighbors, listening for the gifts and calling of the staff and ministry leaders, listening to the needs and realities of the community. Listening is not limited to step one before moving on to step two; listening exists throughout the entire process. Anytime we truly pay attention to the movement of the Holy Spirit, we are likely to find ourselves going to places we might never have imagined or predicted. It's not a straight line from here to there.

Throughout the process that Ken and Kay have outlined, there is an interplay between discernment and planning:

listening to the Spirit and to each other in order to map out a path toward the difference God is calling you to make. I encourage you to read the whole book before you jump too quickly to the "how-to's," so you see the many layers and and can build a timeline which allows for both the crucial listening and the essential planning work.

Kay and Ken have given the church a valuable tool in this practical guide to Strategic Planning Retreats. This work is not only important, it is essential for the church today to live into its God-appointed mission. By the grace of God, may it be so!

**Rev. Lisa Greenwood**
Vice President of Leadership Ministry, Texas Methodist Foundation

# Introduction

*If I only had an hour to chop down a tree, I would spend the first 45 minutes sharpening my axe.*

**Abraham Lincoln**

*The block of granite which was an obstacle in the path of the weak becomes a stepping stone in the path of the strong.*

**Thomas Carlyle**

It is one of my favorite things! Yes, that's right. I (Kay) love strategic planning retreats - both participating and leading them. Some people think it is absolutely crazy to love such a thing that others might dread. Why do I love them? There are several reasons:

1. Time away for team building

2. The opportunity to do the "big picture work of the church"

3. Setting strategic direction for the upcoming year

4. A time to renew the leadership covenant

5. Time to evaluate the current state of the church

6. An opportunity for deeper equipping

It is one of my favorite things, too! I (Ken) love strategic planning retreats for all the reasons Kay listed above, and a few of my own:

1. A chance for the leaders of the church to step away from the "whirlwind" of every week in a local church to get up in the "balcony"

2. A time of learning and growing as church leaders

3. A chance for us to hear, maybe in a new way, where God is calling our ministry

## Importance of Retreats

*Give us clear vision that we may know where to stand and what to stand for—because unless we stand for something, we shall fall for anything.*

**Peter Marshall**

We strongly believe that growing and vital congregations find strategic ministry planning not as "another thing to do," but rather the essential foundation built each year to set the most faithful path forward to fulfill the Great Commission - to go and make new disciples. We feel the Great Commission is not merely a nice thing to do or a suggestion. Instead, we feel this is what every church MUST do! Strategic ministry planning is the best step to make sure we are constantly and consistently working on our disciple-making mandate.

We believe the essentialness of the annual strategic planning retreat is directly connected to the effectiveness and fruitfulness of the ministry of your church in the upcoming year. Strategic planning retreats are both important and essential in the life of the church. Given our belief of the non-negotiable need for an annual strategic ministry planning retreat for the leadership team, we continue to be astonished at the number of churches who do not pursue nor complete this essential work. Or maybe if there is planning completed, it is "completed" in a couple of hours on a Saturday morning. If there is no retreat, the church is simply not being strategic about its future and its focus on its purpose of making disciples. If there is a very limited time of strategic planning, it is most likely mere calendaring and not strategic planning.

Please allow me (Kay) to share a metaphor I often use in training and coaching churches. Imagine a ship out at sea bobbing around, enjoying the perfect temperatures and bright sunshine. There are the faithful crew members swabbing the decks and polishing the brass railings. Great pride is taken in caring for the ship. Down below, there are talented crew members cooking up yummy casseroles and desserts for everyone on-board to enjoy. As the clouds move in, the sea becomes a bit rough and waves begin to lap up over the sides of the ship. The crew members work harder and swab faster.

As the waves become larger and more frequent, those polishing the brass begin to help those swabbing the deck to stay ahead of the waves slopping up onto the deck. Before the crew knows it, the clouds have turned into a storm and the cooks must be called up on deck to help bail water to keep the ship afloat. The whole crew becomes afraid the ship will capsize in the turbulent waters caused by the storm. Friends, this ship is like many of our churches.

7

Good faithful people love their church. They work hard to maintain the facility and conduct all the "traditional" ministries. Yet, everyone is so busy swabbing the decks, polishing the brass, and cooking the casseroles that we are not paying attention to the highest priority of work of the crew (church). The crew (faithful church volunteers) has become too entrenched in "doing" church, and they forget how to "be" the church.

You see, no one had even noticed the motors were not running. No one was steering the boat. No one was in the crow's nest looking ahead. No one was using the GPS to chart our journey and destination. No one was watching the radar so we could steer around the storms. The church was simply bobbing around at sea, allowing the sea to toss and turn the boat into this direction or that, as we are busy playing church. And this has all happened without us even noticing.

Most churches have not intentionally turned off their engines. Most churches have not intentionally failed to chart their course. Most churches have not intentionally failed to plan. Most churches have not intentionally neglected any faithful duties. It simply just happened. Slowly, over time. It has happened because we have not had to be as intentional in days gone by as we are now faced with the need to do in today's and tomorrow's church. By and large, the faithful people working hard in their churches are doing exactly as they were taught to do. Because most churches were not focused on the mission, the members were taught that discipleship was coming to weekly worship, putting a check in the offering plate, and donating items when asked (i.e. canned goods, coats, socks, cookies, etc.). And people did as they were asked and taught to do. They were faithful. They met those expectations. And, this worked when we lived in a church-centric world. When our world was church-centric, people were driven into the church by culture and the church was the center of many people's lives. But in today's non church-centric world, culture is driving people away from and out of the church, and therefore church is the center of fewer people's lives. To be a post-modern church living on its mission to make disciples of Jesus Christ, we must be more intentional and strategic to reach new people. Just bobbing around at sea is no longer enough and no longer effective. We must engage the motors, program the GPS to our agreed upon destination, continuously monitor the weather radar, keep someone in the crow's nest to look ahead, and have someone steering the boat. And all of this cannot be completed in a couple hour-long meetings every month or so. We must plan a chunk of time away to intentionally and strategically plan for the mission before and ahead of us.

## Importance of Strategic Ministry Planning

*Therefore, my brethren, be steadfast, immovable, always abounding in the work of the Lord, knowing that your toil is not in vain in the Lord.*

**1 Corinthians 15:58 (KJV)**

"What does strategic planning have to do with ministry or churches? Isn't that a business process? I don't think all this focus on strategic planning has any place in the church world!"

Those are just a couple of the typical comments we receive as we work with pastors and church leaders. Before we go there, let's take a quick look at what is happening in our churches.[1]

- The median church in the U.S. has 75 regular participants in worship on Sunday mornings, according to the National Congregations Study (NCS).

- For years, the Gallup Research Organization has come up with a consistent figure - only 40 percent of all Americans said they attended worship on the previous weekend. Another resource suggests this number is greatly inflated and indicates less than 20 percent of Americans attend church regularly.[2]

- The median church attender age is 73 years old. The median age of the total population in the U.S. is under 40.

- In America, 3500-4000 churches close their doors each year and half of all churches in 2008 did not add one new member through conversion growth.

- The largest generation in our country right now is the millennials, those born between 1980 and 2000, numbering over 78 million. Roughly 85 percent of them are unreached.[3]

---

[1] From the Hartford Institute for Religion Research. http://hirr.hartsem.edu/research/fastfacts/fast_facts.html. Accessed February 13, 2020.

[2] *Outreach Magazine.* ChurchLeaders.com. April 10, 2018. https://churchleaders.com/pastors/pastor-articles/139575-7-startling-facts-an-up-close-look-at-church-attendance-in-america.html

[3] Thom S. Rainer and Jess W. Rainer, *The Millennials: Connecting to America's Largest Generation.* B&H Publishing Group. Nashville, 2011.

We don't share these statistics with you to be negative, but for us all to realize where we currently stand in our churches. The Christian church in this country is 50+ years past the time of just putting up a sign out front or starting a new additional worship service and having people show up each Sunday. Unfortunately, most pastors and church leaders are unclear about what to do differently.

Let's bring this closer to home. How about your church?

- Look back at the last 20 years of attendance. Have you been growing in worship attendance? Small groups and/or Sunday school classes? Number of people working in hands-on mission?

- What percentage of your membership roster attends worship regularly (at least 1-2 times per month)?

- How many funerals have been conducted of member/attenders?

- How many adult baptisms have you done in the past five years? Infant? Youth? Adult?

- How many millennials do you have involved in the life of the church?

- What was different on December 31st at your church from the previous January 1st? What did you accomplish?

- Is everyone in the church busy doing "church work" but not really advancing the Kingdom? (i.e. making disciples)

- If your church was to close its door today, what impact would it have in your community? Who would call to complain? Who would miss you?

Now let's get back to the questions and comments we receive from church leaders concerning strategic planning. Our basic responses to these challenges rely on scripture.

**Read Acts 2,** and you will discover the core values of the early church.

**Read Matthew 28:19-20,** and you will find the mission statement, Great Commission, for all our churches.

**Read Exodus** to see many examples of God and Moses casting vision.

**Read Nehemiah** to find a great picture of total strategic planning.

There are, of course, many other examples throughout the Old and New Testaments of leaders casting vision, establishing goals, assigning tasks, measuring results, etc. The bottom line? Strategic planning started with the church!

Somehow, we have let the business world take it from us and now too many church leaders view it as secular instead of the spiritual way God clearly intended it to be. Now is the time for us to take back strategic planning, not to be like businesses, but to be like so many of the great leaders throughout the Bible.

## An Outsider

*To me thinking outside the box means; crossing
disciplines and pulling in expertise and perspective
from outside of the standard boundaries.*

**Dror Benshetrit**

One last question we hear from some church leaders is
"Can't we do all this on our own?" Our answer is always,
"Of course," followed by the question, "How has that been
working for you up to now?" Church leaders, much like
everyone else, sometimes need a person from outside the
group to help guide them along the way, make recommendations, and hold them accountable. This is one of the roles
of a good church consultant, coach, or a trained facilitator.
This is someone who can conduct the training and walk
beside the leadership team and pastor as they continue the
process of strategic planning.

Besides the set aside time to retreat for strategic ministry
planning, we believe it is also wise to invite someone outside
the church to lead the retreat. There are multiple reasons
for this recommendation. First, if the pastor or chair/leader
lead the retreat, they are unable to participate.

To lead the retreat puts one in a different role than
participant. Both key leaders need to participate in the
process since they will be two of the key implementers
of the plan. If one of these two key individuals lead, they
could unintentionally steer the group in a preferred direction rather than allowing the plan to unfold from the
group as a whole. These two key leaders need to be able to
completely immerse themselves into the process and not

13

be worried about the details of the retreat, leading, and the agenda. Second, a person from the outside has fresh eyes and ears. Something that has become "normal" for the group may potentially be identified by the outsider as an unknown obstacle or barrier. Third, the outsider comes agenda-free. Each presenter typically brings a unique twist to a strategic planning retreat and therefore allows a greater possibility for innovation and creativity to emerge rather than using techniques that are familiar to the group.

Much like Jethro counsels Moses in Exodus, an outside person can also help point out what needs to be changed to not wear yourself out and to focus more clearly on the vision God has for your church. The outside person has the unique opportunity to be the neutral person in the room who will not be personally affected by a decision or direction considered or planned by the team. Therefore, the outside person can lead from a place of non-anxiousness, neutrality, and keeping the focus of the mission and vision.

We are excited that you are taking this journey of discovery. Our prayer is for you and all the leaders in your church to get in touch with what God has in store for you this year and for years to come.

## Resource Guide

While we strongly recommend someone on the team NOT leading the retreat (someone other than the pastor or team member), we have provided this book as a resource. The goal of this resource is to provide a complete guide to preparing, conducting, and following up afterwards. This resource prepares the team and the retreat leader for the best possible experience and outcome from the strategic ministry planning retreat.

Strategic ministry planning is absolutely critical for effective and fruitful ministries. There are multiple benefits for intentional, strategic planning. Those benefits include:

- **Purpose.** Everyone is on the same page, knowing the purpose of their existence. Each team member knows what direction the church is headed and how they plan to get there.

- **Synergy.** There is synergy when everyone is working together for the same outcome.

- **Easier and Aligned Decision Making.** Decisions are easier to make. If a program or ministry does not fit the goals, mission, and vision, then the answer to start or continue it is a resounding "no." Or at least a grace filled, "This may be something God is calling you to do, but it does not fit into where we feel God is calling the church at this time." Temptations of starting or continuing programs/ministries just because of the tradition or leader's desire are no longer valid.

- **Easier Evaluation.** When there is a mission, a vision, and clear goals, it is much easier to evaluate the overall effectiveness and fruitfulness of the total church and each individual ministry. It is also easier to evaluate the pastor based on ministry fruitfulness (accomplishing the goals) rather than personality or the assessing body's personal experiences with the pastor.

- **Focus.** Because of the intentionality of planning, there is a renewed focus on goals and the resulting outcome at all levels including leadership team, pastor, staff, ministry leaders, teams, and the congregation.

- **Ownership.** When there is a very specific plan of action with goals outlined, it is much easier for leaders and the general congregation to take ownership and grow excited about the future.

- **Momentum.** When everyone is on the same page and pulling in the same direction, there is increased momentum, energy, and excitement for everyone. With this momentum, there is greater movement and aligned accomplishment.

- **Giving.** People get excited about giving to something specific instead of a general budget, salaries, or the light bill. If they can see that they are giving toward a ministry with clear plans for the future, people are more likely to give more. People like to be a part of making something incredible happen.

> *I appeal to you, brothers, by the name of our Lord Jesus Christ, that all of you agree, and that there be no divisions among you, but that you be united in the same mind and the same judgment.*
>
> **1 Corinthians 1:10 (ESV)**

## Five Components of Strategic Ministry Planning

There are five main components of strategic ministry planning. While we are going to cover each of these in detail in *Understanding the Five Elements of Strategic*

*Ministry Planning* section, we thought it would be good at this point to just give you a brief overview of each. Our experience has been that in both the church and the business worlds, many people confuse these terms.

1. **Core Values:** the constant, passionate, biblical core beliefs that drive our ministry.

2. **Mission:** a broad, brief, biblical statement of what the ministry is supposed to be doing. The focus is on "what" we are to do.

3. **Vision:** a clear, challenging picture of the future of the ministry, as you believe that it can and must be. The unique way your church will carry out the mission. God's preferred future for your church.

4. **SMARTER Goals:** tangible measurements on the path to the vision.

5. **Objectives** (aka strategies): the bullet point/actions associated with each goal; what each person or team is going to do to accomplish the goals of the church.

Does your church have any of these already? We would encourage you to have these with you as you work through the process. Please don't worry about or focus on right and wrong, or good and bad. Keep your focus on what God is calling your church to be in the community. You may or may not decide to keep what you have. What we want you to accomplish through this process is for your church to have each of these in place to move you forward as you advance the Kingdom.

## Why this Book

The true potential of strategic planning retreats can pay dividends for a year or more. They set the tone, pace, and focus for the upcoming year. For something this important, it is essential to have a guide to help you and your team have a successful experience. We offer this resource as a guide to prepare, conduct, and follow up for strategic planning retreats. Too often, we have the best of intentions for our strategic planning, but we often find churches and leaders missing elements and opportunities in their strategic planning. Because we have seen the enormous benefits of conducting and participating in strategic planning retreats, we are offering this guide book to you to assist you and your team in having the best experience possible and make the most of your time together to glorify God and make disciples of Jesus Christ for the transformation of the world.

We recommend using this resource as a playbook. Begin preparations in the summertime to ensure readiness for a fall retreat. So, let the journey to a strategic ministry planning retreat commence!

# Understanding the Five Elements
# of Strategic Ministry Planning

Before we head to a strategic ministry planning retreat, it is vital for us to understand each of the elements of strategic planning. It will be important for each retreat participant to be familiar with the elements.

**Note:** It is also important for the participants to be clear about whether the mission is clearly understood and adopted prior to the retreat. Another important part of preparing will be making sure there is a church vision that has been discerned and introduced before attending the retreat. Now let's dive into the five elements of strategic planning.

## First Element: Core Values

*Those who accepted Peter's message were baptized. God brought about three thousand people into the community on that day. The believers devoted themselves to the apostles' teaching, to the community, to their shared meals, and to their prayers. A sense of awe came over everyone. God performed many wonders and signs through the apostles. All the believers were united and shared everything. They would sell pieces of property and possessions and distribute the proceeds to everyone who needed them. Every day, they met together in the temple and ate in their homes. They shared food with gladness and simplicity. They praised God and demonstrated God's goodness to everyone. The Lord added daily to the community those who were being saved.*

**Acts 2:41-47 (CEB)**

*Core values are what support the vision, shape the culture and reflect what a company (organization) values. They are the essence of the company's (organization's) identity – the principles, beliefs or philosophy of values.*

**Nicolas Schoenlaub**

Our core values explain who we are—our identity. They explain why we do what we do. This is true for both individuals and organizations. In churches the core values are the constant, passionate, biblical core beliefs that drive the ministry.

The core values of each church are unique. Think about the answers to these questions:

- What makes us different? (from other churches)

- What is it that attracts people? (or turns them away)

- Why are you at this church?

- What are people here looking for?

Imagine a new couple started attending your church. They came to worship each weekend, got involved in serving, attended classes, etc. They did everything possible on the church calendar. After a month or so you went up to them and asked them to describe your church. The words and phrases they used would be great clues to the core values of your church.

Here is another way to look at core values. In this country we have laws that we are expected to follow and not break. United Methodist churches are expected to also abide by the Book of Discipline for our denomination. While most churches would never consider breaking any laws or going against the Book of Discipline, they are also guided by their core values. Think of these as the guide rails or banks of a river which guide us on our journey toward a destination (our vision – more on that later).

You might also think about your church's core values as the boundaries your church as a whole allows the leaders, pastor, and staff to do ministry within. Even though we find churches often do not name their core values, leaders have "bumped up" against core values with some decisions from time to time. If tradition is a highly held core value of your church, making changes to anything within the church that is deemed and valued as traditional will be difficult. Conflict may arise quickly.

It is my (Kay's) experience that leaders are often way out ahead of their congregation or have not taken the time to get to know their congregation (and the core values) before trying to move the church forward. I once worked with a congregation that identified a couple of their core values as status quo and tradition. But because the newer pastor had been able to navigate some pretty substantial changes, the leadership team created some very innovative and aggressive goals for the upcoming year. When the pastor went back to the church and began working with staff on the objectives to accomplish the goals, there was incredible push-back from the congregation. What happened? The boundaries of the core values of status quo and tradition had been crossed and the congregation claimed the "play" had ended just like when the soccer ball passes over the side boundary on the soccer field. Leaders must clearly identify core values so they know the size of the field where ministry can occur and where the boundaries are of where ministry can happen.

All churches have core values. However, most have never taken the time or effort to identify them. The question isn't do we have values, but which values go deep and really, truly guide what we do?

The early church clearly had core values as we read about in the Book of Acts. The five essential core values of the Jerusalem church were:

1. **Evangelism** (Acts 2:41, 47)

2. **Instruction** (Acts 2:42)

3. **Fellowship** (Acts 2:42, 44-46)

4. **Worship** (Acts 2:42-43, 46-47)

5. **Service** (Acts 2:44-45)

## Second Element: Mission

*Therefore go and make disciples of all nations, baptizing them in the name of the Father and of the Son and of the Holy Spirit, and teaching them to obey everything I have commanded you. And surely I am with you always, to the very end of the age.*

**Jesus, Matthew 28:19-20 (NIV)**

*Every church should have a mission statement and a vision statement. The two are inextricably related but are clearly distinct. Mission precedes vision, but without vision, it is empty and incomplete.*

**George Barna, *The Power of Vision***

*...the church's mission is to make disciples. Thus, the evaluation of the mission demands, Show me your disciples! In 2 Corinthians 13:5 Paul instructs the church at Corinth, "Examine yourselves to see whether you are in the faith; test yourselves."*

**Aubrey Malphurs, *Advanced Strategic Planning***

Mission is what an organization does. Think about a large organization in your community. What is it that organization does? How about churches? What is it that churches do? If we were to look at your website, read your bulletin, talk to your ministry leaders, examine your church newsletter, review your church calendar, and tour your facilities, what might we say is your mission?

In simple terms, churches make disciples. That is what we do. Until you are clear on the mission, you are unable to cast the vision, set goals or objectives in a relevant manner. Each of these items is tied together, but the mission is the starting point. The mission is our clear identity. It is our purpose. It is our why! The mission of the church is a broad, biblical view of the church's purpose. The mission states the intention of the congregation.

In Matthew, it is clear as to why a church exists:

> *Then Jesus approached and said to them, "All power in heaven and on earth has been given to me. Go, therefore, and make disciples of all nations, baptizing them in the name of the Father, and of the Son, and of the Holy Spirit, teaching them to observe all that I have commanded you. And behold, I am with you always, until the end of the age."*
>
> **Matthew 28:18-20 (ISV)**

Jesus was and is very clear, our mission is to make disciples. Many churches will say that in different ways. Some churches have gotten real creative in how they articulate their mission. That is fine, as long as no matter what we say clearly connects back to Matthew 28: 18-20.

In The United Methodist Church, this mission is understood and adopted in many of the local churches. It is the mission statement of the denomination.

> *The making of disciples of Jesus Christ for the transformation of the world.*
>
> **Mission of The United Methodist Church**

It isn't necessary to spend lots of time trying to determine what God is calling us to be as a church. The church is a child of God and is therefore equipped to be the family of God. There are many service organizations serving people with needs. However, what is the difference between the church and other service organizations? God! We serve people in the name of God! We serve people out of our love of Jesus Christ and our desire to teach others about the love and grace of Jesus Christ. This is truly taking ownership of our purpose and what makes us unique. Until we grasp that basic understanding and our responsibility for being a church, we will meander through day-to-day of "doing church" and not becoming the church with a mission.

The mission is stagnant. The mission (purpose of the church) of an organization does not change nor does the mission of a church change over time. We don't expect the Great Commission to change anytime soon! So, we believe that until Jesus comes back to tell us otherwise, we need to not spend another day trying to determine the purpose/mission of our church. Let's do what was told to us in the Great Commission! Unfortunately, we have both discovered how much time churches waste in trying to figure out the mission of the church when it has been given to us. Instead, embrace the mission provided by Jesus and invest the energies instead to living into the mission.

## Third Element: Vision

> *Vision without action is a dream. Action without vision is simply passing the time. Action with vision is making a positive difference.*

**Joel Barker**

*Without a vision of a new tomorrow, we are all inclined to attempt to do yesterday all over again.*

**Lyle Schaller**

*A vision is a clear mental picture of what could be, fueled by the conviction that it should be.*

**Andy Stanley**

*Where there is no vision the people cherish. That is, they cherish something in the church: place, personality, programs or people.*

**Will Mancini**

"What is a vision? Where do they come from? Visions are born in the soul of a man or woman who is consumed with the tension between what is and what could be. Anyone who is emotionally involved—frustrated, broken-hearted, maybe even angry—about the way things are in light of the way they believe things could be, is a candidate for a vision. Visions form in the hearts of those who are dissatisfied with the status quo. . .. Vision carries with it a sense of conviction. Anyone with a vision will tell you this is not merely something that could be done. This is some-thing that should be done."[4]

Mission is what a church does (makes disciples) and vision is where God is calling the congregation to go. While all churches have the same mission, each church's vision will be unique. There are many reasons for this: location, gifts of the congregation, and the needs of the

---

[4] Andy Stanley. *Visioneering.* Multnomah Books. Colorado Springs. 2005, p17.

community, to name just a few. Vision is a discernment process. Vision should always have an element of the future. We are not there yet, but are heading in that direction. We hear God's voice calling us to a new place through prayer, reading scripture, and engaging with others in the community. If a church is not careful, the vision will be what they want and not necessarily what God wants because they are only listening to their own voices.

Vision is not necessarily a statement that has to be easily remembered or able to be put on a bumper sticker. Although many times there are keywords that dominate the statement and can be used as flagship reminders of the statement. These keywords can also be used to name the ministry teams that will lead the congregation in accomplishing the vision. This allows a clear connection of the vision into the action steps of accomplishing the vision through the ministries.

In Thom Ranier's book, *The Breakout Church,* he defines the "Vision Intersection Profile." This is a great self-discovery tool that allows a church to discern the needs of the community, the passions of the leadership, and the gifts of the congregation by using a Venn diagram. For it is where all of these three intersect that the vision of the congregation lies.

## Fourth Element: SMARTER Goals

> *It is not enough to be busy, so are the ants. The question is, what are we busy about?*
>
> **Henry David Thoreau**

*I have so much to do today that I shall spend the first three hours in prayer.*

**Martin Luther**

*Without goals, and plans to reach them, you are like a ship that has set sail with no destination.*

**Fitzhugh Dodson**

Goals are something we want to accomplish. Once we know where we are going (vision), we know what it is we do (mission), and what is important to us (core values), then we need to take a step or two in that direction. That is where goals come into play. While there are many different types of time frames used for goals, from long range of several years to short range of several weeks, throughout this book we are going to focus on the use of annual goals. We have found in our experience that these are the best types for churches to focus on based on how often leadership changes are made in churches.

Churches who set goals are more likely to move toward their vision than those who do not set goals. Goals provide a sense of direction and meaning to ministry teams. Goals have the power to energize and motivate. However, goals that are vague, unrealistic, too challenging, or too easy can actually do more harm than good. Fortunately, there is an easy way to set good goals. The process can be easily broken down into the acronym SMARTER. SMARTER stands for Specific, Measurable, Actionable, Results-Oriented, Time-Based, Eternal, and Recorded. As a leader in your church, it is important for you to ensure the church is using SMARTER goals each year. Let's take a closer look at each of the SMARTER goal areas:

**Specific** – A specific goal is much more likely to be accomplished than a general or vague goal. A key question to answer at this stage would be, "Why should this goal be accomplished?" Keep in mind that simple goals are better. The easier to understand, the easier it will be to communicate and ultimately achieve. In our experience, this is the number one missing element in most goals. Churches or organizations set goals such as, "Do more local service projects" or "Reach more people." These are all nice things. But they are not specific enough. While they may be very specific in one person's head, there is real danger in trying to communicate this with others. One way to help you identify the "why" in your goal is to try starting the sentence with the words, "In order to _____." The words you use to fill in the black will usually help you identify the "why" in your goal. If the "why" of a goal is missing or not clear, then the people who hear that goal will tend to fill in that gap with their own "why" and it is usually very different from than those who wrote the goal.

**Measurable** – All goals need to be quantifiable. This is often a challenge for churches and ministry leaders. We like to argue that doing God's work is not always measurable in human terms and say things like, "We may not have grown numerically, but we are growing spiritually." While that may be true, our experience has been that a tangible measurement of some type is usually available if we work hard enough. We must establish a certain set of criteria for measuring progress toward accomplishing each goal that we set. Questions like the following can help to identify if a goal is measurable: How much? How many? How will I know the results have been achieved? Is there something observable that can be measured? When progress is measured, it is easier to stay on track, reach target dates, and achieve success toward our vision. We count so that we can measure our progress.

**Actionable** – Does this goal strongly suggest action of some type? You should be able to clearly see in the goal that action will need to take place on someone's or some team's part in order for this goal to be achieved. Better yet, reading the goal should move someone or some ministry team toward taking action! A good way to achieve this in the goal statement is to include action verbs.

**Results-Oriented** – Will this goal move the ministry closer to God's vision? No church or church leader needs more tasks to do. We all long to see growth toward where God is calling us. Too often we see fruitfulness and faithfulness as opposite ends of a spectrum, while in God's kingdom they are best viewed as a "both/and" situation. This is never a perfect or easy process for us in the church world. Measuring the right results will help us connect our goals and the results to the vision God has for us.

**Time-Based** – Setting a realistic time frame to accomplish a goal will result in continued progress towards achieving that goal. Even if all of the goals are for the calendar year, you can still break them down into quarterly or monthly steps which will help you gauge progress and make any necessary adjustments to ensure achievement of each goal. Without a set time there is no sense of urgency. You should always be able to write your goals on a calendar. Be careful to never let a deadline for a goal pass. Too often that will lead to a goal never being completed. If a date in a goal is no longer realistic, then leaders should negotiate a new date.

**Eternal** - If this goal is completed as intended, will we feel that we have helped to advance the kingdom of God? This component of the goal is intended as a place for us to check ourselves to ensure we are not just setting a goal to make ourselves happy. In at least some of our goals, there should be space for God to work. In other words, the goal is challenging enough that we cannot currently see how we can accomplish it in our power with our current resources. We need to think BIG!

**Recorded** - There is a great quote from Fitzhugh Dodson, "Goals that are not written down are just wishes." We have all been in meetings where there was great discussion, big decisions were made, everyone felt great about what was going to be done next, but it all sort of fell apart because no one wrote anything down and everyone went their separate ways thinking someone else would let them know what needed to be done. The other situation is where some people remember the conversation one way, and another group of people remember the conversation another way. Remember the telephone game? Writing goals down helps to ensure a common understanding and communication.

This section on SMARTER goals is based on materials from the book, *Time Management for the Christian Leader* by Ken Willard.

## Fifth Element: Objectives

After church goals are set, setting objectives is the next and final step in the planning process. While goals are a means to measure growing closer to living into the vision, the objectives are the actions steps of the goals. It is also a way to drill down the church goals into the goals of the individual ministry team goals. Goals are the major ideas, whereas the objectives are the particulars of who is going to do what to accomplish the goals. Objectives put arms and legs on the goals to create action. The objectives assign responsibility of the goals. The objectives address the who, where, and when of the goals.

# SECTION ONE

## Preparing for the Retreat

*Is there anyone here who, planning to build a new house, doesn't first sit down and figure out the cost so you'll know if you can complete it? If you only get the foundation laid and then run out of money, you're going to look pretty foolish. Everyone passing by will poke fun at you: "He started something he couldn't finish."*

**Luke 14:28-30 (MSG)**

This section of the book is all about what happens prior to the strategic ministry planning retreat. Spanish novelist, Miguel de Cervantes said, "To be prepared is half the victory." The benefit of proper preparation is shown throughout the Bible. Noah prepared for the flood because he listened to God and built the ark. Nehemiah made many preparations before undertaking the rebuilding of the wall around Jerusalem by praying, fasting, and arranging for supplies. Jesus, too, prepared for His ministry on earth by spending time in the wilderness. While some parts of this section may just be good reminders for you, be careful not to go too quickly or to make the mistake of assuming any of these elements are in place only to find out later they were missing or overlooked. The more prepared you are for this journey, the more fruit you and the ministry will see from your efforts. We will look at the following areas in this section:

- Preparing Participants
- Preparing the Retreat Leader
- Preparing and Choosing the Space
- Choosing a Time

## Who Should Attend

*"If your actions inspire others to dream more, learn more, do more, and become more, you are a leader."*

**John Quincy Adams**

Who are the leaders in your church? Who are the people who come to mind first? The Ken Blanchard Company defines leadership as, "the capacity to influence others by unleashing the potential and power of people and organizations for the greater good." Using this definition, who in your church has that capacity? Part of determining who should attend the strategic ministry planning retreat will need to be determined by the role a person holds in the church. For example, depending on the size of your church, there may be one or more pastors in your church. As the spiritual leaders of the church, they should certainly attend the retreat. (Note: we use the term "pastor" knowing that some churches may have an ordained clergy, a licensed local pastor, a certified lay minister, or some other type of person as the spiritual leader. Please translate as needed for your particular situation.) The lead pastor serving in a local church should be included in the strategic ministry planning retreat. Associate pastors may be included in the strategic planning retreat. Often pastors who are not involved in the direct ministry side of the house (i.e. congregational care, finance, facility, etc.) would not be included in the strategic ministry retreat. Have a discussion with the facilitator, pastor, and leadership team chair to determine the best strategy of who should attend if your church has more than one clergy on staff.

Have you ever been to a meeting where there were clearly too many people there? What were the signs you noticed that there were too many people? Maybe it was hard for some people to be heard. Maybe a few outgoing people took control of the meeting and it felt like they were making all the decisions. How about the other side of that coin? Have you ever been to a meeting and it was hard to get any traction because there were clearly some key people not present? The best retreats will have just the right number of people present to ensure the development of a plan for the ministry's future, and not so many people that individuals feel left out or run over. In our experience, that number is usually in the 10-20 range. These are not firm boundaries, but a guide to work with as you consider who should be present. The size of your church will also determine the best number of people. Smaller churches and very large churches may need a smaller group. Mid-size churches may need a bit larger group.

A good starting place for determining who should be invited to the retreat is often the church leadership team which meets every month or so during the year. In many churches this team is called the Administrative Board, Church Council, Leadership Team, or some other such name. Typically, there are people in this meeting representing ministry areas such as finance, trustees, staff relations, children and youth, women, men, Christian education, small groups, and additional areas. There is usually a chairperson for this team and you might also have a church lay leader. Whether your church is using a "traditional" leadership structure or some version of a "simplified" structure, there will be some group of leaders managing the running of the church. We are not suggesting that you simply include everyone who normally attends the monthly administrative board meetings. We are just encouraging you to use that as a starting place.

Many churches will have people who are not currently serving in any form of formal leadership position, but should be included in this retreat. They might be people who have served in the past and have "rolled off" recently. They might also be individuals who for various reasons are not serving in a leadership role now, but you see the gift of leadership in them and feel they will be serving soon. I (Kay) would be careful about inviting ministry team leaders and staff to the strategic ministry planning retreat. In my experience, I find that these folks are ready to get into the "calendering" and planning particular events. This is NOT the purpose or intended outcome of the strategic ministry planning retreat. Instead, this important work will be done as the next step after the strategic ministry planning retreat with the staff and ministry team leaders to develop the objectives to accomplish the goals to live into the vision.

At this point, we would recommend that you create a working list of who should be invited to attend the retreat. Write down each person's name and why (not just their role in the church) you feel they should be a part of this process. Set the list aside for a few days as you pray and listen for God's Spirit to speak to you. There is a very good chance that at least one more name will surface during this time of prayer and discernment. We recommend this discernment being done by the leadership team chair, pastor, and facilitator.

Once you have your list of participants for the strategic ministry planning retreat, a best practice is to personally invite each person. This will give you a chance to explain the overall process and answer any questions they might have. We have found this to be more effective one-on-one and not in a group setting. This will help to highlight the importance of the retreat and to differentiate it from other church meetings. You might even consider having some nice invitations printed and giving each person a copy of this book.

Make sure you provide plenty of advance notice to the participants to be invited to the retreat. People live very busy lives and calendars fill up very fast. If your leadership team is a standing team, you may even set the strategic ministry planning retreat date up to a year or more in advance. This is especially helpful for new people rolling onto the team to know the expectations of serving on the team and planning accordingly.

## Preparing Participants

*He who is best prepared can best*
*serve his moment of inspiration.*

**— Samuel Taylor Coleridge**

Have you ever been to a meeting or gathering of some type and felt unprepared? Maybe you went expecting to be a "wallflower" and just hang out in the background, then someone called on you to share critical information. Or maybe you went to a gathering expecting a boring presentation from a "sage-on-the-stage" and it turned out to be an interactive and inspirational session which provided you with valuable information you could actually use in your ministry. The point is, we all prefer to be prepared and to have some clear expectations for meetings we are going to invest of ourselves to attend. The people who will be participating in your Strategic Ministry Planning retreat are no exception.

There are three ways most people go to a meeting: a vacationer, a prisoner, or an explorer. A vacationer goes to a meeting just wanting to hang out, maybe connect with some people, but mostly just glad they are away from somewhere else for a while. A prisoner goes to a meeting against their will. They feel they are being forced to attend and want to be back home or back where the real work of ministry is being done. An explorer attends a meeting anticipating to learn new ideas, see something in a fresh way, and become better equipped to lead their ministry to produce fruit for God's Kingdom. As a facilitator, you will need to understand these three ways people might attend your retreat and encourage everyone to be an explorer. Consider how you as the facilitator and pastor can help prepare participants so more might show up as explorers. This can be accomplished by considering who is invited and what preparations are done with participants ahead of time. Superior communications can also be helpful to create more of an explorer attitude.

There are three main areas included in preparing participants: prayer, reading, and homework. We will cover each of these in detail shortly. Before we get to those areas, there are a couple of key things for you to consider as you, the facilitator, prepare for the retreat.

- Who will be attending? For you to best prepare your participants, you will need to know who they are and their roles in ministry. This includes the simple information of name, position, and email, but also goes beyond this data. How long have they been in this role? Have they been included in any prior strategic ministry planning with this church? Another church? Another setting (i.e. corporate)? What do you need to know about each person that you might not know already? Gathering information about your audience is a critical component for the success of the retreat.

- How and when will you communicate with the participants? Once you know who will be attending the retreat, it is time to put together a communication strategy. As the facilitator of the retreat, it is important for you to consider your audience and their needs above your own preferences. For example, you may like to send out email communication, but then discover that several participants prefer phone calls over emails. The following is a sample communication strategy. You will need to adjust the timing, communication vehicle, and frequency to the needs of your participants and each retreat you facilitate.

- Once the retreat is booked and the participant list created, an email is sent out to the whole group welcoming them to this process. Included in the email is all the logistical information they need, (dates, address, times, etc.) along with clear instructions concerning any pre-work they will need to complete prior to the retreat. Also included in this email is a link to a short online survey they need to take today. (See Appendix I.)

- Consider adopting a guiding scripture or two for the retreat. Work with the pastor to discern what would be helpful to guide the team in their preparation and prayer. Communicate the scripture to the participants, including why the scripture was chosen and how it relates to the upcoming retreat.

- Depending on the date of the retreat and the date of your first communication to the participants, we recommend some form of short communication every 30 days. This communication may just be an email reminding them of the upcoming retreat, the pre-work they have been asked to complete, and to continue praying for God's Spirit to guide the whole process.

- A couple of weeks prior to the retreat we recommend a short, no more than 30 minutes, video call with the whole group. (You may want to use a service such as Zoom for this communication.) We have found that some form of "face-to-face" at this stage can help the participants see themselves as a team and increase their level of commitment to the process. Use this time to remind everyone about the logistics of the retreat, check in with them on the pre-work, and answer any questions which may have come up.

- During the week leading up to the retreat, if possible, set up a text group which includes all of the participants. Send the group a text letting them know you have created the group and encourage them to use this for any last-minute questions and to communicate with you and each other concerning the retreat. If text will not work for you or your participants, you may need to substitute email or phone calls.

- The day before the retreat, send the participant group one last communication, (text, email, or phone) focused mainly on prayer for your time together.

## Prepare by Praying

> *Rejoice always, pray without ceasing, give thanks in all circumstances; for this is the will of God in Christ Jesus for you.*

> **1 Thessalonians 5:16-18 (NIV)**

As stated above, there are three main areas we encourage you to include in preparing the participants for the upcoming strategic ministry planning retreat: prayer, reading, and homework. The first area we will cover is prayer. Jesus said in Luke 11:9, "So I say to you: Ask and it will be given to you; seek and you will find; knock and the door will be opened to you" (NIV). Prayer is not just a motion for us to go though, it is critical in this whole process! There is a very real danger as we begin to discern the future for a ministry—if we are not listening to God's Spirit in this process, then we are listening to our own wants and desires. Too many churches have gone down the path of doing what makes those who are already there happy and content only to close themselves off to both their community and to God. We encourage you and everyone who participates in the strategic ministry planning process to be serious about prayer and not just go through the motions. We would like to share with you some best practices concerning prayer in this process for you to consider and pray about.

**The first best practice for prayer** in the strategic ministry planning process we encourage you to consider is beginning and ending everything in prayer. You can start this with your very first communication to the participant team and continue it through your final follow-up post retreat. Each time the group gathers, has a phone call or video conference, and even your conversations with individual leaders, begin and end with prayer. To state the obvious, this does not need to be only you doing the praying, it can and should include the whole group of participants. A short prayer at the beginning and another short prayer at the end of all sessions can help to center everyone, including you, and keep the focus on God's will and desires for this ministry. Begin and end everything in prayer.

**The second best practice for prayer** in the strategic ministry planning process we encourage you to consider is establishing prayer partners within the group of participants. Take the list of participants and in partnership with the lead pastor, pair up each person on the list with a prayer partner. Communicate with the whole group who they have each been partnered with and encourage them to meet at least weekly before and after the retreat to share any prayer concerns they may have individually, to pray for the process, and for the leaders to clearly discern God's voice for the future of your ministry. Be careful not to assume everyone has done this type of prayer partnering before; you and/or the pastor may need to share more information.

**The third best practice for prayer** in the strategic ministry planning process we encourage you to consider is utilizing the church's prayer team, prayer list, or any other current methods of prayer. Many churches have a prayer system already in place which you can tap into for support in this overall process. In our work with churches, we often encounter a prayer system which is totally focused on the people already somehow connected to the church. Take a look at the worship bulletin or other prayer list the next time you are in a church. Please hear us clearly: praying for church members, families of church members, etc. is not bad. It is a wonderful place to start. However, we are encouraging any church in the process of strategic ministry planning to take this opportunity to expand the circle. Pray for the overall strategic ministry planning process, pray for the leaders involved in the process, pray for the person facilitating the process, AND those in the church's mission field who are far from God, those who have been hurt by the church, those who have never heard the Good News, the de-churched, the un-churched, all the names and labels we use for God's lost sheep. This is a perfect season to grow the church's prayer ministry!

> *Wherever you go, I'll give you that land, as I promised Moses.*
>
> **Joshua 1:3 (NIV)**

**The final best practice for prayer** in the strategic ministry planning process we encourage you to consider is called prayer walking. If you have not done this before, it is exactly what it sounds like--praying while you walk. As you can tell by now, prayer and discernment are a major part of any good strategic ministry planning process. One of the best ways we have found to really hear something new from God is to get out into the community God is calling us to serve and listen for God's Spirit to speak and observe what God is showing us with new eyes.

Most of us are creatures of habit. We shop at the same stores, eat at the same restaurants, take the same routes to and from work, and associate with the same people as we have for years. Thus, many of us think we know our communities much better than we really know them. What we really tend to know is our small section of the world around us. God is calling us to more. God wants each church ministry to reach and serve the whole community, not just our small part. Prayer walking is a powerful way to open a group of church leaders up to the new things God is up to all around us.

**See, I am doing a new thing! Now it springs up; do you not perceive it?**

**Isaiah 43:19a (NIV)**

Early in the process of preparation for the strategic ministry planning retreat, cover prayer walking with everyone who will be a participant in the process. (Some churches may want to include other people from the church in the prayer walking part, which is great of course, just emphasize that it should not be in place of those leaders who will be participants.) The following are some sample instructions you might share with the people who will be prayer walking. We encourage you to adapt them to your specific situation.

- Many people have only experienced the prayer posture of head down, hands folded, eyes closed. While this is the most common posture of prayer in our culture, the Bible tells us of people praying while standing with arms raised, and people praying while prostrate on the ground. The point is, all postures of prayer are acceptable to God, even praying with our eyes open as we walk.

- Each local church congregation is called to be a life-saving station to the community all around them. Our church building is a launching pad for our ministry in our mission field. For the local church leaders to properly discern where God is calling them requires getting out of the building and into the community - the mission field.

- The objective of prayer walking is to better hear from God's Spirit and to see our mission field with God's eyes. This takes time and intentionality. While a person can always drive around the community while praying, (as long as they keep their eyes open!), we have found that driving is too fast. Walking causes us to slow down and gives us time to best see and hear what God wants us to in a new way. Those who are going out to prayer walk should go with the expectation that God is going to show them something new, and God's Spirit will speak to them during their walk.

- Imagine the mission field for the strategic ministry planning participants as a map. Maybe it is a one-mile radius around the church building, or maybe a certain zip code or school district, or maybe it is a certain section of city blocks. Now envision slowly highlighting that whole mission field map with color markers to indicate where people from the congregation have prayer walked. (We have worked with churches who have done exactly this activity.) What a powerful visual to indication covering the community in prayer!

- We have found it best to send people out in pairs to prayer walk. This is for safety, and to give people an opportunity to be together as they hear from God and see new things together. If there is anyone in the group of leaders who is not physically able to prayer walk, please be sure to find a way to include them in this process. Like the other leaders, they should not do this alone. In fact, you may want to encourage prayer partners mentioned before to prayer walk together.

- Expect for people to be moved to tears and for people to return from prayer walking in need of sharing what they saw and heard from God. A pastor or other well-equipped leader should be in place and available every time people go out into the community to pray. We know of one Sunday school class who went out on a prayer walk around their church and the whole group came back in tears. There should also be some way to record the words, phrases, images, etc., people are receiving from God's Spirit.

Two other books to go deeper in this process of prayer walking are *Flood Gates* by Sue Nilson Kibbey and *Stride: Creating a Discipleship Pathway for Your Church* by Mike Schreiner and Ken Willard.

## Prepare by Reading

> *Reading is essential for those who seek to rise above the ordinary."*
>
> **Jim Rohn**

The second area for preparing your participants for the upcoming strategic ministry planning retreat is **Reading**. We have found that most leaders we work with are readers. So, asking your participants to read a book or two prior to the retreat should not be a problem. Having each leader who will participate read at least one book will enable you to take advantage of some common language and points of reference. This means choosing a book or books, and asking each leader to read the same book(s). How much you ask the group to read prior to the retreat will certainly depend on how many days there are between when you meet, when you give them a reading assignment, and what prior equipping will be helpful to the participants and the retreat experience.

There are a couple of different approaches to choosing which book(s) the group will read. The first approach is to pick a resource that is broad in scope and yet has a strong connection to the overall strategic ministry planning process. Examples might include books like *Canoeing the Mountains* by Tod Bolsinger; *Kingdom Collaborators: Eight Signature Practices of Leaders Who Turn the World Upside Down* by Reggie McNeal; *Simple Church* by Thom S. Rainer & Eric Geiger; *The Purpose Driven Church: Growth Without Compromising Your Message & Mission* by Rick Warren; or *The Emotionally Healthy Church: A Strategy for Discipleship That Actually Changes Lives* by Peter Scazzero.

The second approach is to choose a resource which is specifically about strategic planning overall or at least one of the components. Examples might include books like *God Dreams: 12 Vision Templates for Finding and Focusing Your Church's Future* by Will Mancini; *Ministry Nuts and Bolts: What They Don't Teach Pastors in Seminary* by Aubrey Malphurs; or *Choosing the Faithful Path* by Beth M. Crissman. New books are released every week. We are sure you have some of your favorites, too. The point here is not as much about which book(s) you use, but more about the advantages of having the leaders who will be participating in the retreat to spend time reading a book or two.

# Prepare Through Homework

*You will never get anywhere if you*
*do not do your homework.*

**Jim Rogers**

The third area of preparing your participants for the upcoming strategic ministry planning retreat is **Homework**. There are four aspects of homework in preparation of the retreat: self-study, values survey, guiding principles, and mission field analysis. Each of these will play a part in the actual retreat in separate but connected ways. The completion of each area of homework will need to be done far enough in advance of the retreat to allow time for the leader and the participants to review the findings and have time to process the information in a discerning manner. We encourage you to not rush this part of the process.

**The first area of homework** prior to the strategic ministry planning retreat is what we refer to as a self-study. We have included an example of a local church self-study in Appendix II. Instructions for the self-study are also included in that Appendix section. The purpose of this activity is for the church leaders to come to the retreat with a clear picture of where their ministry has been in the past and where it is currently. Having an accurate picture of current reality is extremely important for the participants to have. This self-study will take most churches three to four months to complete. It is not intended to be something the church rushes to complete or does haphazardly. The findings from this activity will be a key part of the foundation for the entire planning process. No matter the size or type of church completing the self-study, it is best done in sections with a person or team taking responsibility for each section. There should also be one key leader, pastor, or maybe the administrative board chairperson, who is overseeing the whole activity to ensure everything is completed and returned on time. The retreat facilitator will need a copy of the total completed self-study along with the responses of each participant to the leadership questions in Section 8.

**The second area of homework** prior to the strategic ministry planning retreat is a core values survey. Administering the core values survey prior to the retreat time will allow the participants to have this information available to them for discussion and discernment. Appendix III shows an example of a core values survey. The church pastor(s) and leaders will need to decide on a final listing of core values to include in the survey, how the survey will be administered and to whom, and the timing of the survey. We covered core values in great detail in the Understanding the Five Elements of Strategic Ministry Planning section of the book. The following are our recommendations for the core values survey.

- Chose a listing of 20 to 30 values. There are many sources and examples available; you will just need to do a little research to determine a listing more appropriate for your ministry. Feel free to use the sample we have in Appendix III as a starting point. We have found short descriptors helpful when listing the values. You should not need to explain or define the values too much.

- Depending on your audience and situation, you may find it beneficial to set up an online values survey. This can be very helpful in compiling your results. However, a paper survey will work also. You also need to determine your audience for the values survey. We recommend giving the whole church an opportunity to complete the survey. This is more challenging than just asking your leaders or retreat participants to take the survey, but it will give you a more accurate picture of the total ministry and not just a few people. As you will see through the rest of this book, much of the overall strategic process involves a small part of those attending the church (mostly leaders). Asking everyone who attends the church to complete the values survey is a great way to include more people in the overall process, and let them feel they have a voice.

- We recommend having the congregation complete the core values survey as soon as possible. There is no reason to wait. Take a look at the church calendar once you begin the journey toward the retreat and find a week or two which will work best in your ministry. In our experience, churches have seen high completion rates when the pastor spends a few minutes in a worship service giving an overview of the strategic ministry planning process--defining values--and explaining the survey. If the church is doing an online survey, then the link should be in the worship bulletin or made available in some other way. If the church is doing a paper survey, then we recommend handing them out right after worship and asking people to take a minute right then to fill it out and turn it in. A good participation rate to aim for is 60-70 percent of the church's average worship attendance. In order to reach that goal, the church may need to repeat this process two or three times. We do not recommend extending the survey for more than four weeks, unless you have some type of unusual circumstances, as the percentage of people completing the survey does not tend to increase much after the first couple of weeks. You will also need to be careful people understand they should only complete the survey once.

Once the surveys are completed and the results tabulated, you will need to narrow the list down to a manageable amount. A total list of somewhere between four and eight core values are most common in churches. The list of top values from the survey may be very different than what the leaders of the church would have identified. This difference may help you see potential areas of disconnect, or areas where there is an opportunity to better communicate or focus.

For example, church leaders may feel "accountability" is a value, but it scored very low in the survey. The congregation might feel it is an issue, and church leaders might not feel that way. This could be an opportunity to go deeper and ask some follow up questions to a congregation focus group. Another area to keep in mind is what is commonly referred to as "aspirational" values. These are the values that the church is aspiring to, but are not yet in place. The church leaders may want "evangelism" or the reaching of new people to be a value, but it may not show up very high on the survey because it is not yet in place. In some cases, a value such as "evangelism" will show up very high on the survey, but the actual results do not support the claim that the value is actually in place. Values which are claimed, but not supported with fruit or results may also be seen as aspirational. We have found it helpful to sometimes include one aspirational value in the final listing, as long as everyone is clear that it is a value not yet achieved, but a work in progress. Remember also, these should be core values of the church/congregation, not core values of individuals. While the values of the church may certainly change over the course of time, the final list you create through this process should last for many years.

Having a list of great core values is not enough for any organization. They must be demonstrated through the way the organization behaves. There was an example of this many years ago. Do you know whose core values these are: excellence, respect, communication, and integrity? Did you guess Enron? (If you are not familiar with this organization, it would be worth looking them up.) While the core values of a church should be there to guide us, they should also be visible to others in how we behave.

**The third area of homework** prior to the strategic ministry planning retreat are guiding principles. Guiding principles are broad philosophies which encompass the church's values and help to guide the organization through its ministry. While they are sometimes written, they may also be those unwritten rules that everyone is expected to know. A church's guiding principles become a part of the culture and indicate what is most important. An example of a guiding principle in a church could be the rule that any spending by a ministry of over $250 at one time, even if it is within their budget, must be approved first by the finance chairperson or the treasurer. These guiding principles can be thought of as the boundaries which ministries should not cross as they make disciples. Our mission is to make disciples of Jesus Christ. So, keeping the rules is not the objective of the game, but how we play the game. As we make disciples, we should of course not break any federal, state, or local laws. If we are a United Methodist Church, we should not knowingly do anything against the Book of Discipline. And finally, there are the rules, policies, and guiding principles of our church.

Each participant of the strategic ministry planning retreat should be provided a copy of any church guiding principles. The homework is to review those guiding principles and make notes of questions, and identify opportunities for discussion. In the case of a church not having any guiding principles written down, then as homework each participant should create a list of any guiding principles they feel are already in place, and a list of potential guiding principles they feel may need to be created to help, not hinder, the ministry of the church. The purpose of this activity is to better equip the ministry leaders to make disciples, not to add more rules or punishment.

**The fourth and final area of homework** is mission field analysis. The leadership team needs to have a clearly defined mission field. In other words, what area around the church is God calling the church to reach? It might also be stated as the area of the neighborhood which the church is willing to take responsibility for reaching the souls who reside there. We have to stay away from thinking of our mission field as only the area in which our current attenders live. This is especially true when the church has become a drive-in church; members drive back to the church that sits in the neighborhood they used to live in until they moved away. The neighborhood where the church sits is the neighborhood the church is called to reach. If the church is unwilling or unable to reach its neighborhood for Jesus, the church needs to either relocate or turn the keys over to a congregation who is willing to reach the neighborhood.

Once the mission field parameters are identified, demographics need to be gathered. This information includes but is not limited to population trends, average age, ethnicity, socioeconomics, education, household size, professions, marital status, etc. Experian offers demographic information details by segments called Mosaic types. This Mosaic information is invaluable. It identifies a particular lifestyle segment and details how this particular segment lives in detail such as how old they are, what they drive, what kind of jobs they have, what they like to do in their spare time, how the play, their digital preferences, reading preferences, what their dreams are, and so much more. We highly recommend the leadership of the church discerns which Mosaic type living in the church's mission field will be identified as the people God is calling the church to reach.

Knowing who the church is called to reach will be

extremely important before heading to the strategic ministry planning retreat. Too often we have worked with churches who create goals that will never be reached because they are identifying goals to fulfill making disciples from a demographic who does not live in the mission field. Or worse yet, we are too scarcity-minded and therefore try to do all things to reach all people and in the process reach no one because we have no focus, priority, or resources to reach everyone.

Let me (Kay) offer an example of this disconnection for your consideration. I was working with a church who had been doing an after-school ministry for school-age children for nearly 20 years. The group who was once more than 50 children was now struggling to reach six children. The faithful leaders worked harder and harder to tweak the ministry to try to attract more children. But the result was tired volunteers and no more children. When we looked at the demographics, (Specifically, the demographic tool we used was MissionInsite.) we discovered that the school-age population had very sharply declined over the past decade and the population of 65+ had dramatically increased. This tired team was trying too hard to reach one of the smallest populations in their mission field and were completely overlooking the largest demographic population. And, interestingly enough, the team was made up of the 65+ age population. They were relieved to know that it would be perfectly okay to discontinue the school-age ministry which had a decreasing need and population, and, instead use their resources and energy to reach the demographic they were most familiar with - people like themselves!

Until the church identified the change in their mission field and gave the team permission to shift their focus, the team felt as though they were failing in ministry. Now, the team had a new spark of energy creating new strategies to reach this new demographic who were their neighbors.

## Preparing the Retreat Leader

*Success occurs when opportunity meets preparation.*

**Zig Ziglar**

We know that in some cases the person reading this book will be the retreat leader. Earlier in the book we shared why a church needs to use an outside leader to lead the retreat. So, we will not cover that information again here. Our focus in this section will be on how to best prepare the retreat leader. When we use the term "retreat leader" in this section we are referring to the person who will interact with the participant group by asking questions and helping the group discover and discern their own way forward, guided by the Holy Spirit. While a small amount of teaching and training may take place during the retreat, the leader will primarily be facilitating the movement of the group forward to their goal of strategically planning their ministry for the upcoming year.

Just as the participants will gain more from the retreat by being properly prepared, so too will the retreat leader perform their role by being as prepared as possible. The following are our recommendations for the retreat leader in order for them to be properly prepared going into their time with the participants.

- The retreat leader should have a copy of this book and read it well in advance of the retreat.

- This is a season for the retreat leader to intentionally take a step in their prayer life. As disciples of Jesus, we are all on a journey of sanctification. Steps forward on this journey happen best with some intentionality. While growing in all areas of spiritual disciplines are important, the time leading up to the retreat is an important time to focus on the discipline of prayer. Each of us are in a different place on our journey, so it would be impossible for us to say exactly what the appropriate next step would be for any individual. We would encourage the retreat leader to meet with someone who could coach them to discover the best next step for them in the area of prayer.

- The retreat leader should read and be familiar with any books the participants are reading in preparation for the retreat. They will also need to be clear on how those books will be used and referenced during the retreat. This may require them to produce some type of materials or to create an activity of some type to be completed during the retreat. For example, the book *God Dreams* by Will Mancini contains vision examples and templates the leader might want to have copies of, or maybe 3 x 5 cards created for use during the retreat.

- The retreat leader should read and be familiar with all homework the church and the participants have completed in preparation of the retreat. The amount of data and information can become overwhelming in some cases. The leader must be able to absorb the information and discern important trends by seeing the whole picture and not "getting lost in the weeds."

- The retreat leader should be in consistent communication with the local church pastor throughout this process. A good rule of thumb would be for the pastor and retreat leader to talk live, on the phone, or via video conference at least twice a month leading up to the retreat. These do not need to be long conversations, just long enough to ensure everything is moving forward smoothly and any questions or issues are being addressed.

- While it would be good for the retreat leader to worship with the church at least once, tour the facilities, and drive around the local community prior to the retreat, we understand this may not always be possible based on where the retreat leader lives and the location of the church. This might be a good bonus for those retreat leaders who do live close enough to the church to make this possible.

- The retreat leader should also be as familiar with the retreat location as possible. Especially in relation to the setup of the space and technology. A well-planned strategic ministry planning retreat will not have any surprises, for the participants or the leader. Time and effort invested ahead of the retreat by the leader will ensure a more fruitful and productive experience for everyone.

## Preparing and Choosing the Space

*May the God of hope fill you with all joy and peace
as you trust in him, so that you may overflow
with hope by the power of the Holy Spirit.*

**Romans 15:13 (NIV)**

While many churches have adequate space to host the strategic ministry planning retreat, we strongly encourage you to find a location somewhere away from the church facilities. Being on-site at the church will usually have too many distractions for this process to achieve its full potential. We have found great benefits from asking the participants in this type of a retreat to spend a couple of nights away from home, even if the distance is commutable, so that everyone can really immerse themselves into the process. As most things in this section, you will need to filter all of our suggestions and recommendations through the lens of your reality and possibilities.

Here are a few things to look for in a good location for your strategic ministry planning retreat.

- Space for everyone to sit comfortably. A main room which allows you to configure the setup, table and chairs placement, to best suit the size of the total group and the facilitator's preferences. An optimum table and chair arrangement for this type of process is a large "U" with the participants around the outside and the opening of the "U" facing the front of the room. This allows everyone to see and hear each other, and the process facilitator to be in the middle. Be sure the chairs you use will be comfortable for people to sit in for an extended time. (No metal folding chairs!)

- Accessible for everyone. Before choosing a final location for your retreat you will need to understand the accessibility needs of your participant group. Some accessibility needs may be obvious, but others will require some investigation. There are too many possibilities for us to adequately cover them here. Please check with each participant before you choose a location concerning their physical, dietary, sleeping, and any other types of requirements they might have to best accommodate them during the retreat.

- Technical equipment. Are you going to use a PowerPoint presentation at any time during the retreat? Then you will need a projector, a screen, a computer, and electrical power for everyone. Many locations now have large TVs instead of a projector and screen. No matter what system you use, be sure all of the participants will be able to see, and maybe hear if you are using sound, comfortably from where they will be sitting. Don't forget to have any necessary cables or cords for the equipment.

The following are some areas to include in your preparation and planning of the location space.

- Plan ahead for meals and breaks. You do not want to break the flow of the session by having to stop and figure out meals and breaks, nor do you want to have to travel for meals. If you are doing an off-site retreat in a location without food service, you will need to arrange

61

for everything ahead of time including plates, utensils, drinks, etc. Preparing quick meals and cleaning up can be shared by prayer partner teams as an added time together with prayer and team building. One church we worked with had someone secretly contact each participant's spouse or best friend, and when everyone arrived at the retreat there was a gift bag waiting for them with some of their favorite snacks.

- Depending on the location of your retreat, you may also need to plan to have a work team prepare the space and return for cleanup. While most participants would be happy to help with these chores, it is always a nice touch to have these chores done by another team.

- Don't forget about elements such as sleeping arrangements (including potential linen needs) if you are staying on-site somewhere, and emergency contact numbers for each participant.

- We recommend starting each day with a short worship service. Prayer, scripture, and an upbeat worship song or two are great ways to center the group for the day ahead. Someone will need to ensure these are ready to go before the dates of the retreat. A best practice is to ask a pastor and worship leader from another local church to come in each morning to lead worship. We also recommend ending the overall retreat with communion. Arrangements will need to be in place for the elements to be delivered at the appropriate time.

- No matter how well everyone in the group knows each other, we have found it helpful to start these retreats with some type of team building exercise or maybe a quick ice breaker. These are great ways to get people energized and talking each morning of the retreat. They do not need to be too elaborate or involved. Focus mainly on having some fun and getting to know each other a little more.

- The retreat should be a "phone-free" zone. Our mobile devices are so much a part of our lives today that it can be a real challenge for us to step away from them for any period of time. However, this type of planning retreat requires our total focus so that we can best hear God's Spirit speaking to us about the future of our ministry. A best practice we have seen is to place a basket at the front door for everyone to place their phone in when they enter. Clearly communicate to everyone when they will be able to check their phones (lunch, breaks, etc.), so they are best able to concentrate on the purpose of the retreat. Be sure to communicate this expectation to your participants well ahead of time.

## Choosing a Time

> *Time is free, but it's priceless. You can't own it, but you can use it. You can't keep it, but you can spend it. Once you've lost it you can never get it back.*
>
> **Harvey Mackay**

The timing of the strategic ministry planning retreat will depend on factors such as the size of the church, the availability of the participants, and many other factors. For example, a church where most of the participants are retired, the retreat may be conducted during the week because they are available at those times and the pastor can still preach on the weekend. A church with only one service on Sunday and where the majority of their leaders work in the community during the week would need to conduct the retreat on the weekend. There is no "one-size-fits-all" answer to the timing of this retreat. Having said that, here is our recommendation for a strategic ministry planning retreat based on our experiences in leading countless retreats:

- **Friday 6pm to 9pm** - The group can start with dinner. (It is always good to break bread together.) There will then be time to begin the retreat process before calling it a night.

- **Saturday 9am to 5pm** - This is the main day for the retreat process.

- **Sunday 9am to noon** - This is when the retreat process moves into the actions and next steps planning.

Starting on Friday night allows time for the participants to "turn off" their work week before you jump into the main section of the retreat on Saturday. We will cover the agenda in more detail later in the book. Having the retreat conclude on Sunday morning can be a good strategic choice. This will ensure all of the church leaders are focused on the retreat process the whole time and not on the worship service at their church. Extending the retreat into Sunday also clearly articulates the value of this process so much so that the pastor is out of the pulpit to tend to this important work with the leadership team.

The other aspect of choosing a time is what part of the year you want to hold your retreat. The weather in some areas may play a part in this decision, but we are really referring to the church calendar. Consider the cycle of the year in your church. When are new leaders coming on to the administrative board or church leadership team? When are you preparing your financial budget for the next year? For many churches, but maybe not all churches, an early fall retreat would work best. For churches running a fiscal year of July 1 to June 30, you might want to consider a retreat in the February to March time frame. Keep in mind the need to consider the time needed for ministry staff to work on objectives/strategies and subsequent budget requests, and the final budget approval by the leadership team before year-end or judicatory deadlines.

# SECTION TWO

## Conducting the Strategic Planning Retreat

*As iron sharpens iron, so one
person sharpens another.*

**Proverbs 27:17**

All the preparations are complete and the retreat is now upon us. It is time for us to come together collectively to discern the direction of our church for the coming year. It is both an exciting and anxious time. As the retreat facilitator, be prepared for retreat participants to arrive with a variety of emotions and expectations no matter how much preparation has been done. Remember, some participants have never had a retreat experience before. Others have just worked a full week at their corporate job that was stressful. Some come with burdens around family relationships and/or other family burdens. And still others have been looking forward to this experience since they were first invited.

Remember, you will likely have vacationers, prisoners, and explorers all attending the retreat together. Knowing all of this, prepare a welcoming environment that is inviting and puts people at ease as much as possible as soon as possible.

Here are some tips to consider:

- Make sure everyone has very clear directions to the retreat center. Nothing is worse than getting lost on the way to the retreat to build up frustration and tension prior to arrival. Some may even car pool. Use signage if it would be helpful and is appropriate on the route to the retreat location.

- As facilitator, arrive early so everything can be set up ahead of time. This allows you to not be rushed or tense before leading this important process for the participants. In addition, you are then freed up to greet everyone upon arrival rather than still being in setup mode.

- Prepare name tags in case not everyone knows one another.

- Have refreshments available upon arrival.

- Have sleeping room assignments completed ahead of time and communicated to the participants. Make sure participants know if they need to bring bedding, towels, and/or soap/shampoo with them or if it is provided.

- Make sure the participant arrival time is scheduled 30 minutes or more before the anticipated retreat start time. People will want to get settled in before getting started. Invariably someone will be late, too.

- Consider creating a participant "goodie bag." This might include a pen, notepad, special snack, journal, mints, bookmark with church vision, and notes from the church prayer team, prayer partner, and/or pastor.

## The Main Purpose

*Your purpose in life is to find your purpose and give your whole heart and soul to it.*

**Buddha**

There will be several elements/parts of the strategic planning retreats. Each part has a unique and important purpose. The portions of the retreats could be identified in three main categories:

- Review and Discovery
- Goals
- Next

Again, each of the categories are important and should not be skipped. At the same time, it is important to understand that the meat of the retreat is the setting of the goals. The "review and discovery" as well as "next" may look different each year depending on the life of the congregation, but the goals are essential. The goals provide the direction for the upcoming year for the entire church: pastor, staff, leaders, teams, and congregation. Too often we leave goals to the end of the retreat or do not allow enough time. When this occurs, we either walk away with no goals, weak goals, or incomplete goals.

Make sure everyone understands this is the heart of the retreat and needs the most time and attention. The review and discovery steps will help inform the goals and is therefore an important step in the process. The next step is again important, but should be informed by the goals set.

In order to help identify the different categories of the retreat, please see the agenda in the upcoming pages of this section broken down by the three identified categories.

## Getting Started

Gather the participants in a room that has adequate space for people to move around and one table large enough to accommodate everyone following the recommendations in the previous preparation section. Depending on how well all the participants know one another (or not), plan introductions, team building, and/or ice breaker activities. Ask each participant to share their expectations about the retreat along with their prayer preparation experience. Capture their expectations on flip chart paper.

Next, share the agenda and schedule including meal times and daily start and end times with the participants. You might even agree upon a break schedule such as (for example) trying to break about every 90 minutes or so. Or maybe there are no scheduled breaks other than meals so everyone is welcome to use the facilities or fill drinks at their leisure. Everyone is more comfortable when they know what to expect, so investing time in setting expectations will pay dividends for the retreat overall. If a guiding scripture was chosen for the retreat, make sure it is posted at the retreat.

Spend some time reminding the participants why this particular scripture was chosen and how it relates to the work ahead of the participants during the retreat. Ask participants to share what God has revealed to him/her through their prayer time regarding this guiding scripture. If appropriate and relevant, capture these insights on flip chart paper and post them in the room to remind the participants of what God revealed during the participants preparation time leading up to the strategic ministry planning retreat.

> *Clean living before God and justice*
> *with our neighbors mean far more to God*
> *than religious performance.*

**Proverbs 21:3 (MSG)**

Establish the covenant for the retreat. The covenant might include agreed upon cell phone usage, covering the process in prayer, being fully engaged, being open-minded to the process and one another, fully participatory, etc. It is important to talk about establishing a safe space so people will feel comfortable being very open with thoughts, feelings, and ideas. Establishing an atmosphere where brutal honesty is not only safe, but expected and valued is imperative. Capture the covenant on large newsprint and keep it posted throughout the retreat. We would also encourage the participants to sign the covenant as a sign of acceptance to the agreed upon covenant. Make sure someone is taking notes to capture the happenings during the retreat.

## The Agenda

Here is an agenda for your consideration. Feel free to edit it to fit your context, needs, and duration of the retreat. Keep in mind, however, the elements listed in this agenda are pretty much the basics. For this reason, most activities on the agenda should not be excluded, while other elements may be added. These might include music, time spent with prayer partners, times of silence or silent prayer for discernment, more worship, or other pressing work for the leaders.

### Discovery and Review

- Prayer
- Introductions
- Group Covenant
- Year in Review
- Mission Field Review
- Core Values
- Mission
- Vision

### Goals

- SMARTER Goals

### NEXT

- Strategies
- Guiding Principles
- Spiritual Development Needs for Upcoming Year
- Leader Development Needs for Upcoming Year
- Closing Worship and Communion

The first three elements of the agenda (prayer, introductions, and group covenant) were covered under the previous Getting Started section of this section. We will now unpack each remaining element on the agenda.

## Year in Review

> *For now we see in a mirror dimly, but then face to face. Now I know in part; then I shall know fully, even as I have been fully known.*

**1 Corinthians 13:12 (ESV)**

Before we move forward, it is best to have a clear grasp on where we have been and our current reality. Here are some recommendations on how to bring the participants along in this task.

- First discuss what the leaders believe is driving the church. Is the church being driven by the vision? Relationships (internal and/or external)? Ministries? Structure? If you are unfamiliar with these terms, research the Bullard Church Lifecycle and refer to Chapter One of *Gear Up* by Kotan. If it is determined that vision is not driving the church, there may need to be some re-visioning done before the retreat. Visioning as a possible step prior to the retreat was discussed in the earlier preparation section. Where is the church in its life-cycle? What do we need to notice or know from this exercise? What course corrections, if any, need to be made? How does this information and discussion inform our strategic planning work and planning ahead of us?

- Next, let's look at our current year's goals. What is our progress? What can we celebrate? Where did we see gaps? What can we learn from this review? How does this review inform our strategic work and planning ahead of us?

- Take a look at your church statistics over the past year. You may find it helpful to include the previous three to five years of statistics to identify larger/longer trends. These include average worship attendance, adult professions of faith, baptisms, numbers in discipleship groups (i.e. small groups, Sunday school, etc.), stewardship, number of first-time guests, number of returning guests, numbers involved in serving, and others your church may be working to improve such as number of children and youth involved in ministry. What trends are you noticing? What trends call for celebration? What trends need course corrections? How will these statistics and trends inform our strategic work and planning ahead of us?

- Capture the participants' learnings on flip chart paper to post and reference for the duration of the retreat. Make sure this work is also captured in the minutes of the retreat.

## Mission Field Review

> *So reach out and welcome one another to God's glory. Jesus did it; now you do it!*
>
> **Romans 15:7 (MSG)**

Churches often find themselves thinking they know their mission field when in reality they have lost touch with their neighbors. This is especially true if a great number of attendees do not live in the mission field. Instead, they drive into the church on Sunday and "do life" in another part of town or maybe even a completely different town/city. Your church is located where it is to serve the people who live around it. If your church doesn't reach them for Jesus, then who will? We (Ken and Kay) believe our church is called to take responsibility for the souls in your mission field. This was discussed in the previous preparation section and was identified as part of the homework to prepare the participants for this discussion.

The church needs to be the community expert. That is, know the neighborhood (aka mission field) better than anyone else. How can we reach people unless we know who they are, what keeps them up at night, and their hopes and dreams? Most churches have access to demographic information that is full of all the information you need to understand and fully know your mission field. We are most familiar and use the demographic provider called Mission Insite (https://missioninsite.com/). Regardless of which provider you use to gain access to the information, it is important to review this information at least annually.

Take a look at trends such as population, ethnicity, age trends, socioeconomics, employment, housing, poverty, etc. What trends are you noticing that are changing? Is your congregation a representation of your mission field? Who is your targeted Experian mosaic segment? What must your church do to reach this mosaic? How does this review inform the strategic planning ahead of you? [5]

---

[5] For more information, see http://business.library.emory.edu/documents/databases/simmons-mosaic-usa-descriptions.pdf.

Capture the mosaic segment the church is targeting to reach on flip chart paper for the duration of the retreat. Select three to five key identifiers of the targeted mosaic segment, too.

> **Note:** Depending on how much time is set aside for the retreat and what other work needs to be completed during the retreat, this may be work that is completed ahead of the retreat.

## Core Values

> *And whenever you stand praying, forgive,*
> *if you have anything against anyone, so that*
> *your Father also who is in heaven may*
> *forgive you your trespasses.*
>
> **Mark 11:25 (ESV)**

Does your church have identified core values? If so, post them on the flip chart paper to remind the participants and keep them in front of the group for reference throughout the retreat. Now compare those existing core values to the homework the congregation did around core values. What core values are the same? Which are different? What changes in your current (reality) core values need to be made? What aspirational values will help grow the church into God's preferred future for the church (aka vision)? What, if any, core values are working towards achieving the vision and which ones are working against the vision?

Remember, core values (existing and aspirational) determine the size and boundaries your church can work within to achieve the mission and vision. Capture the current and aspirational values on flip chart paper for the duration of the retreat for reference. Also capture this information in the minutes of the retreat.

## Mission

> *Jesus, undeterred, went right ahead and gave his charge: "God authorized and commanded me to commission you: Go out and train everyone you meet, far and near, in this way of life, marking them by baptism in the threefold name: Father, Son, and Holy Spirit. Then instruct them in the practice of all I have commanded you. I'll be with you as you do this, day after day after day, right up to the end of the age."*

**Matthew 28:18-20 (MSG)**

You will remember from the earlier section *Understanding the Elements of Strategic Planning,* we (Ken and Kay) believe the mission has been given to us by Jesus Christ. The mission of every church comes from Jesus' words, the Great Commission, printed above.

We have both worked with churches who spend months, if not years, trying to figure out the mission of the church. Spend no more time! Jesus clearly told us why the church was created. Know it. Own it. Focus on it. Prioritize it. All the church does should lead towards fulfillment of the Great Commission. How will reminding ourselves of the church's purpose inform our strategic planning? Write the mission on the church on flip chart paper and post it for the duration of the retreat to remind us of our purpose. As leaders of the church, **you are responsible** for leading the church in its mission of making disciple-making disciples.

## Vision

> *"For I know the plans I have for you," declares the LORD, "plans to prosper you and not to harm you, plans to give you hope and a future."*
>
> **Jeremiah 29:11**

Vision, as covered thoroughly in the previous preparation section, is the unique way your church accomplishes the mission of making disciples. Vision is God's preferred future for the church. The vision comes from the intersection of the needs of the community, the gifts of the congregation, and the passions of the leaders. As leaders of the church, it is necessary to monitor the vision consistently. Is the current vision driving the church? Have the needs of the community changed? Have the gifts of the congregation changed? Have the passions of the leaders changed? Anytime any of these three have changed, the vision is no longer driving the church, and/or the church needs to start a new life-cycle; a new vision must be cast.

The strategic ministry planning retreat is based on planning towards achieving the mission of making disciples through the church's unique vision. Before the annual strategic planning retreat, it is best to discern if the vision will carry us faithfully through another year of revisioning.

At the retreat you might identify that vision is waning and revisioning needs to be done in the upcoming year, but the current vision can be used for the strategic plan until the new vision is discerned. For the purposes of this retreat, capture the current vision statement on flip chart paper and post it for the duration of the retreat to remind the team of where God is calling to church for the future.

## Goals

*May he give you the desire of your heart and make all your plans succeed.*

**Psalm 20:4**

*My goals exceed the reach of my energies, but my God exceeds the reach of my goals.*

**Craig D. Lounsbrough**

Given the work completed by the retreat participants at this point, it is now time to begin working on goals. The goals need to be based in what the church must do in the upcoming year within the boundaries of the values to achieve the vision (God's preferred future) of how the church uniquely lives out the mission (its purpose) to make disciples. All the work done up to this point was to help better inform what direction the church should be headed in the upcoming year.

Have the participants get up and move around the room reviewing all the information captured on the flip chart paper thus far. Offer a prayer asking for discernment, clarity, and God's guidance for this next crucial step in the strategic planning. It may even be appropriate and/or needed to spend some time in silence, prayer partner time, or even prayer walking before taking this next critical step. Try to wipe the slate clean of all the church is and does right now so that new direction can be discerned for faithful next steps in fulfilling the mission and vision. This is not the time to protect pet projects, favorite people, sacred cows, and "the way we've always done it." This is instead a time to being completely open to the Spirit moving and obedience.

Gather the participants once again around the table. Ask each participant to *briefly* recap what they are discerning about what the church needs to be doing in the upcoming year so that the vision becomes more of a reality. Remember these are big-picture steps, not individual ministry area ideas or objectives (day-to-day activities). Instead this is the big ideas that will lead to what needs to happen in day-to-day activities so that we live into the vision. Capture these big ideas on flip chart paper.

Note: If you have some participants who might not feel comfortable speaking up in the group or if there is some tension or a hard shift that needs to be made, consider doing this exercise by having each participant write down their big ideas. Gather all the lists and the facilitator will write them on the flip chart paper. As facilitator, you would then read them aloud to the group. You will need to discern which direction is most appropriate for the group on the spot.

Once everyone has had a chance to share their thoughts, ask the group to identify any trends in the discerning and recaps. What is floating to the top? Where do they feel God is calling them in the upcoming year? What feels like the next few faithful steps? Begin to identify the top three to five areas to work on. The number will depend on the capacity of the congregation, complexity, time to complete the potential goal, and the resources needed. Capture the three to five topics identified for goals placing each separate topic on a flip chart page by itself.

Next divide the group into the number of teams equal to the number of goals to be worked on. You might ask if anyone has particular interest or energy around a particular area so they can work in that area. Watch for diversity in the groups as they form.

Give the groups up to an hour to work on creating a smart goal around the area identified. Review how to create a SMARTER goal and refer them back to the earlier section of SMARTER goals in the Understanding the Five Elements of Strategic Ministry Planning. Remind them this is not about "planning events," but rather the "big idea."

Caution them not to veer their work into objectives. This is not their work. Ask the work teams to capture their SMARTER goal on flip chart paper and be prepared to share it with the group at the designated time.

Bring the group back together. Have each work team share their SMARTER goal with the rest of the retreat group. The rest of the group is to "audit" the goal making, to be sure it fits the SMARTER definition, it captures the essence of the team's discernment, and the goal will indeed help the church live into its mission and vision. Make appropriate edits and additions as needed.

Celebrate this hard, holy work!

## Objectives

*All who have accomplished great things have had a*
*great aim, have fixed their gaze on a goal which was*
*high, one which sometimes seemed impossible.*

**Orison Swett Marden**

Objectives (aka strategies) reflect the day to day ministries that will be planned and implemented so that the goals are accomplished. Remember, this next work is not for the leadership team. This is the work for the staff (paid and unpaid staff) and ministry leaders. The only reason this is on the agenda is to remind the participants that this is the next step in the strategic ministry planning process. The budget work cannot be completed until the objectives/strategies are created, budget requests are made, and then either approved or shifted. Remember, if the objectives cannot be completed within the available budget (as discerned by the leadership team), the goals may need to be edited by the same leaders who attended the strategic planning retreat.

## Guiding Principles

*Guiding principles are a set of policies and procedures*
*which allow the ministry of the church to function on*
*a day-to-day basis within healthy boundaries. These*
*principles are permission-giving strategies that protect*
*the overall health and well-being of the church.[6]*

**Kotan & Bradford**

---

[6] Kay Kotan and Blake Bradford, *Mission Possible*. Market Square Publishing. Knoxville, 2019. p 85.

Guiding principles are policies and procedures which provide permission for day-to-day ministry to occur without having to constantly ask (and wait for) leadership approval. The retreat setting is a perfect time to review the guiding principles in their entirety (that is, if the church currently has guiding principles).

What needs to be revised or updated in the current guiding principles? What's missing? What needs to be removed? Are all employee, safety, technology, safe sanctuary, building, financial, and security policies and procedures up to date? For more information on guiding principles refer to *Mission Possible* by Kotan.

## Spiritual development needs for upcoming year

> *The secular mind and heart, however gifted*
> *and personally charming, has no place in*
> *the leadership of the church.*[7]

**J. Oswald Sanders**

What are the spiritual leadership needs for this group? Where would they like to dive deeper? What spiritual practices would they like to improve upon in the coming year? What topics are of interest? Have each person write an idea or two on a piece of flip chart paper. This is now the list of topics that will be used in the leadership team's upcoming meeting for spiritual development. Have each person sign up for teaching one of the topics and assign them a month.

---

[7] J. Oswald Sanders, *Spiritual Leadership: A Commitment to Excellence for Every Believer,* Moody Publishers, 2017.

## Leader development needs for upcoming year

*Leadership and learning are
indispensable to each other.*

**John Fitzgerald Kennedy**

How are we developing and pouring into our existing
leaders? What leadership topics would be helpful in equipping the leaders to lead the church for this coming season?
What leadership topics would be helpful for the team
to study together to strengthen their leadership in the
church? Have each person write an idea or two on a piece
of flip chart paper. This is now the list of topics that will be
used in the leadership team's upcoming meeting for leadership development. Have each person sign up for teaching
one of the topics and assign them a month.

## Reflection Time

*Follow effective action with quiet
reflection. From the quiet reflection will
come even more effective action.*

**Peter Drucker**

Before moving into the closing, ask each participant to
reflect on their retreat experience. Ask them to each offer
one word as a reflection of their experience. Again, capture
these words on flip chart paper. Compare these against the
hopes identified at the beginning of the retreat. Use the
hopes versus reflections as a way to summarize expectations versus outcomes and celebrate the hard, holy work
this team has accomplished. Consider how the participants

might share their experience with the congregation so the congregation can be in continued prayer for the upcoming year of ministry and be informed about the direction of the church as the leaders have discerned.

## Closing Worship and Communion

> *While they were eating, Jesus took bread, and when he had given thanks, he broke it and gave it to his disciples, saying, "Take and eat; this is my body." Then he took a cup, and when he had given thanks, he gave it to them, saying, "Drink from it, all of you. This is my blood of the covenant, which is poured out for many for the forgiveness of sins.*
>
> **Matthew 26:26-28 (NIV)**

As the retreat comes to a close, have the prayer partners spend some time together in prayer for the upcoming year, the goals that have been identified, and the work ahead for the staff and ministry leaders on the objectives/strategies and budget requests. While the participants are spending time in prayer, set up for closing worship and communion.

Place the goals and other flip charts you feel are appropriate on the altar along with any other items of significance. This is the offering/the work given to God. Be sure to tie in the guiding scripture, mission, vision, values, and goals into the closing message. Feel free to ask participants to assist with worship. We suggest having the participants serve one another communion as a closing. Worship is sometimes very meaningful done outside (or another place besides the table they have been sitting at for the retreat) and/or in a circle so everyone is facing one another. Close

with prayer. We suggest a prayer chain where each participant adds to the prayer and then finishes with all participating in the Lord's prayer together.

Note: Be prepared for emotions to come out at the closing
worship. We (Ken and Kay) have both experienced this. A
strategic ministry planning retreat is such a beautiful, holy,
and exhausting experience that participants many times find
this to be a moving, spirit-filled, and a defining moment in
their faith/spiritual leadership walk.

# SECTION THREE

## Following Up After the Retreat

*It takes a leader to create the momentum, it takes a vision to direct the momentum, it takes a massive action to build on the momentum, and it takes self-discipline to sustain the momentum. Momentum is the bridge between a vision and its results.*

**Farshad Asl**

Have you ever set a New Year's resolution? How did that go? If you were able to keep it all year long and achieve that resolution, you are in a very small minority. Visit just about any gym in early January, then go back in March and see the difference. That is a good visual of how people often set resolutions and goals. They are serious at first, but not so much later.

Too often, in our experience, the churches who have gone to the trouble of setting goals for their ministry treat the retreat or goal-setting process as an event. Their whole focus is on coming up with the goals. They will celebrate getting the words just right. And then move on to the next event on their calendar.

You can probably guess what happens when churches set goals and then lay them aside. Like anything in ministry, goals need attention. Trees need water, sunlight, and good soil in to produce fruit. The goals we set during the strategic ministry planning retreat will need care and attention in order to produce fruit for God's Kingdom.

In this section, we will look at what needs to happen after the retreat in order to achieve the goals and keep the ministry moving forward. This is not intended to be a checklist where you do one item then move down the list. As you will see, many of these will have some overlap, while some of them are ongoing in nature. Please read through this section in its entirety, then design and develop a follow-up plan specific to the needs of your ministry context.

## Communication

> *The single biggest problem in communication is the illusion that it has taken place.*
>
> **George Bernard Shaw**

One of the first things that should be done post-retreat is for the leaders to develop a plan to communicate the goals to church. This communication plan will likely include at least three groups of people:

- Ministry leaders who were not present at the retreat
- Influential members of the congregation
- The whole congregation

In most cases there will be a few ministry leaders who were not able to attend the retreat. They will need to be brought up to speed concerning the retreat, especially when it comes to understanding the goals. Emphasis should be placed on why these goals were chosen, and what is expected of them and their ministry areas in order for the church to accomplish them.

This should be more of a discussion and conversation than lecture. The best situations occur when a goal is shared, and ministry leaders are able to determine ways they and their ministry can help the church achieve that goal. A key part of this conversation must be how each ministry will be doing things differently in the future, in order to ensure the goals are achieved. New results require new actions. Doing everything the same way will only produce the same results as the past. A key question might be, "What needs to stop?"

The next group includes influential members of the congregation. These individuals may not have any official leadership roles in the ministry, but they clearly have influence in the church. Most churches will have a small group of leaders they would put into this group. We encourage you to meet with this group after you have met with any ministry leaders who were not able to attend the retreat, and before you communicate the goals to the whole congregation. The purpose of this meeting is not to get their approval, but to inform and allow them to ask questions.

Start the meeting with a brief overview of the whole strategic ministry planning retreat, then focus on how and especially why the goals were chosen. Keep the session as interactive as possible by asking questions and allowing the group to ask questions.

- What excites you about these goals?

- Which of these goals do you feel especially connected?

- When you first heard these goals, what challenged you?

This should not be a "dump" of information. Be sure to give them clear opportunities to be involved in achieving the goals for the church. Influential members can help best when they are not on the sidelines just watching or giving money, but when they are actively involved in goal achievement.

The third group we will focus on as part of the post strategic ministry planning retreat communication plan is the whole congregation. As you reflect on the overall strategic ministry planning retreat, consider what information everyone who calls your church home would benefit from knowing. The answers will be different for every church. Here are a few best practices we have seen:

- A series of short videos on each element from the strategic ministry planning retreat. One video could be an overview with definitions of terms/elements and the rest would then be specific to the church.

- Printed material in the form of an annual report, much like many businesses produce each year, but with information from both the strategic ministry planning retreat and the completed self-study. This would provide members of your church with reading material to take home.

- A sermon series done on each of the main elements of the strategic ministry planning retreat, culminating with a message on goals. Be sure to include your church's new goals for the year. As you have seen, each element in the pre-work and retreat has a clear connection to scripture.

- An all-church meeting after Sunday worship where some of the participants in the strategic ministry planning retreat share each of the elements, learnings from the pre-work, and then announce the new goals for the year. A pocket-sized, laminated card with the goals is then given to each member with extras available to new people who join the church during the year.

While it may be challenging in some situations to make a clear connection between each member of the church and their roles in achieving the new goals, each individual does need to know what those goals are and why they were chosen. We have found that the communication of church goals can impact how people feel about the overall ministry. People like to be a part of something that is growing and planning for the future. We recognize there may be other groups who should be part of the goal communication plan. If this is true for you, we encourage you to identify them now and invest the time to create the proper communication strategy.

## Creating Objectives

*Objectives: This is where the rubber hits the road. Objectives are where the goals grow hands and feet.*

**Kotan and Bradford, *Mission Possible***

After the goals for the church are set, creating objectives – strategies or action steps – is the next phase in the planning process. While a goal is a way to measure our success in growing closer to living into God's vision for the ministry, the objectives are those actions steps necessary to reach each goal. The objectives most often appear as a ministry or event, but may also be a facility project, a new hire, a change in position, or even launching something brand new.

In their book, *The Four Disciplines of Execution,*[8] the authors use the terms *lag measures* and *lead measures* to explain the differences between what we are calling goals and objectives. In essence, goals are lag measures, typically seen after the fact. For example, if my goal is to lose weight (not a SMARTER goal, but one that most of us can relate to), when I step on the scale, the results (the numbers on the scale) are a *lag measurement* because by the time I see them the performance that drove them is already done. *Lead measures* in this example would be things like calorie intake and exercise. *Lead* measures are those things we over which we have some control. These will influence the *lag measurement,* our goal. An example might be worship attendance. The leaders might set the goal to increase average worship attendance. That is a *lag measurement.* By the time you see those numbers, the work to make that happen has already been done. *Lead measures* in this example might be include the number of bridge events to reach new people, marketing efforts in the community, or a sermon series on evangelism.

---

[8] Chris McChesney; Sean Covey and Jim Huling, *The Four Disciplines of Execution,* Free Press, 2016.

Setting clear objectives for each goal is a way to simplify the church goals, creating tangible tasks and action steps for each ministry. Goals are the major ideas. Objectives are the particulars – who is going to do what in order to accomplish the goals. Objectives put the arms and legs on the goals to create action. The objectives assign responsibility of the goals. The objectives address the who, what, when, and where of each goal. In our experience, there are usually some leaders in each church who really struggle with setting goals and seeing them through. These are often the same leaders who will get excited about creating objectives for each goal. For them, this is where the real work takes place in ministry. You can usually identify them in the goal setting process because they want to jump immediately to the objectives and not "waste" time on setting clear goals. Be sure you keep these leaders engaged at every step and use their gifts at this stage to take the goals down into to bite size action steps.

It is imperative goals be worded correctly, in ways that clearly communicate to a wide audience. They should be formatted in the SMARTER framework. Objectives should be more concise and to the point. The objectives for each goal should become the checklist for each person and/or ministry of what needs to be accomplished, by whom, and when. We encourage you to think in terms of bullet point statements.

The objectives can also be seen as the internal, behind the scenes actions, of the out front goals. While the goals should be in place for a year or so in most cases, the objectives should change and be updated throughout the year as things change in ministry. A challenge we have often seen when leaders get to this stage is that objectives are still too large. In other words, the objectives should be broken down into smaller components. A best practice is to write a goal on the top of a white board or flip chart paper, then start writing objectives under that goal. Once you have a good list of objectives, pick one of them and write it on another board. Next, start breaking it down into smaller, very specific steps. This will help you determine how detailed and specific the action steps under each goal will need to be in order for each ministry, leader, and servant to be clear on their roles.

Please allow us to offer a specific pathway to create the objectives to best ensure the goals are accomplished in your church. We recommend the pastor call the church staff (paid and unpaid staff and ministry team leaders) together very soon after the strategic ministry planning retreat. The pastor would want to schedule as soon as the strategic planning retreat is scheduled. A best practice is for this a full-day (or longer) retreat away from the church. The pastor will lead the retreat, working on the objectives as well as building and equipping the team.

The pastor will want to spend some discernment time between the Strategic Ministry Planning Retreat and the Staff Retreat to break down the goals between various ministry areas and staff members. There may also need to be some consideration for adding another team or ministry area if this is needed for the goal accomplishment.

- Which area of ministry will each particular goal be accomplished through?

• Which ministry area will be assigned which goal?

Too often we jump into creating objectives before we establish which ministry will be held accountable for each goal. Also keep in mind there may be a particular goal that will be the responsibility of multiple ministry areas/ staff members rather than just one area of ministry. It is important for the pastor to have this discernment work completed before walking into the Staff Retreat. Without being completed ahead of time, the Staff Retreat could become cumbersome and overwhelming.

At the Staff Retreat, the pastor starts by leading any team building and equipping exercises that will benefit the staff. Next, share the goals and unpack why each goal was chosen. Be sure to remind the staff how each goal will move the congregation closer to its vision of fulfilling the mission. Then share which ministry area(s) will be responsible to accomplish each goal, explaining why they were chosen. Once the goals have been "assigned" to the various ministry areas/leaders, the staff will spend time with their individual ministry area to begin creating objectives to accomplish each goal. The pastor will roam from staff member to staff member, answering questions and offering feedback.

After the Staff Retreat, staff/ministry team leaders will gather their ministry teams together to do further work on the objectives, finalizing the ministry plan for the upcoming year. The final step in this phase of planning is for each ministry team, under the direction of the staff/ leader, to create a budget for their ministry area to support the goals assigned through the objectives.

The pastor then reviews all the objectives and budget requests and tweaks as necessary with staff member/ministry team leaders. The pastor assembles the budget requests and presents them to the finance committee for final approval.

Keep in mind, if the budget is not approved, either the objectives and/or goals will need to be adjusted so that all (goals, objectives, and budget) are in alignment. This is an extremely important step in the Strategic Ministry Planning Retreat follow-up. Too often we find the budget is completed outside the Strategic Ministry Planning process and is not aligned with goals created by the ministry teams.

Note: In our experience we often find a lack of alignment when a committee-driven traditional structure is in place. When the council/board is a separate committee from finance, trustees and staff-parish relations, we find committees work with a limited scope, authority, and responsibility for the mission of the church. Instead, their work is often focused in their specific area of responsibility, rather than holistically focusing on how each part of the strategic ministry plan (mission, vision, core values, goals, and objectives) are supported through accountability. If you would like more information on how a simplified, accountable structure can more easily align your church in its mission, please check out Mission Possible by Kotan and Bradford.

## Accountability

> *Do you really want the mission to succeed? Are you prepared to stake everything, change anything, and do whatever it takes - even if it means altering long and familiar habits, redeploying precious programs, and redeploying sacred assets?*

**Tom Bandy,** *Foreword Winning on Purpose*

In order for a church to accomplish the goals to more fully live into the vision (God's preferred future for the church) and to accomplish the mission (to make disciple-making disciples), it is imperative to hold one another accountable through this entire process. In our experiences, churches often struggle with this. We sometimes convince ourselves that holding one another accountable is not what church is about. Because we are a people of grace, we have come to believe that grace-filled means not holding one another accountable. We would challenge this thinking and this way of leading in the church. We believe there is no greater place or no greater need in the church to hold one another accountable! If your church is struggling with accountability, we highly recommend the book, *Winning on Purpose,* by John Edmund Kaiser. It is a great resource to explain accountability in the church context and how to live into it.

So, who holds who accountable? The board/council is accountable to Christ for the church being on mission to make disciples. I (Kay) find that when we talk about the church board/council being accountable to Christ for making sure the church is living out its purpose of creating disciple-making disciples, it causes leaders to pause and reflect on their leadership with a different perspective. Too often leaders in the church find themselves making decisions based on actions that will cause the least amount of resistance (or conflict) rather than what is most effective at making disciples. We often value maintaining our relationships with one another more than our responsibility to Christ to lead the church in its mission.

The pastor is held accountable by the board/council for the vision and goals. This is done at the monthly board/council meetings when the pastor reports the progress on goal accomplishments. This is the place where progress should be celebrated. This is also the time and place for encouragement and questions. For example, if progress is stalled, the board may ask the pastor how the board can be helpful. What is getting in the way of the goal accomplishment? What resources are needed? Too often laity are uncomfortable asking pastors these questions. But to be in church leadership, we must take the responsibility and authority for leading the church in its mission, so we must do our part in holding one another accountable. This includes the pastor.

The staff (paid and unpaid) and ministry leaders are held accountable by the pastor. We often hold church staff meetings and report on all the activities under our given area of ministry responsibility. Too often, we do not tie all the church activities into our mission, vision, and goals. The pastor holds each staff member accountable for executing the objectives identified at the beginning of the year, possibly adjusted along the way, so the goals are accomplished. This is likely done one-on-one with staff members and the pastor monthly (or quarterly) depending on context, staff performance, and depth of goals and objectives. The same sort of questions and feedback the board/council uses with the pastor is used with the staff and ministry leaders.

Ministry teams are held accountable by the staff and ministry team leaders. We need to move away from hiring staff to "do" ministry for us, and instead see staff as equippers and coordinators of ministry. This allows staff the time and energy to help ministry teams work on the best alignment of the ministry teams to achieve their goals, ensuring the objectives are being executed with excellence and alignment. When ministry teams understand how their part of the ministry connects with the larger church ministry, team members are much more passionate and motivated. They feel valued and validated in both their ministry and their accomplishments. They see how they are contributing to the greater purpose of the church. Some of the same questions used with the board/council and the pastor are used with teams.

The staff and ministry team leaders also have other areas of accountability. First, they should make sure each team understands how each ministry, activity, and event in the life of the church within their area of responsibility is connected to the mission, vision and goals of the church. Next, each ministry team needs to know the purpose of the activity or event and the intended outcome. For example, the concert the church is hosting is meant to build relationships with the unchurched people in our neighborhood. The intended outcome is to have 200 people attend the concert, collect 50 new names and follow up, with two new families becoming involved in the life of the congregations within 90 days.

The purpose (evangelism, in our example) and intended outcome (two new families become involved in the life of the congregation within 90 days) must be crystal clear from the beginning. If the purpose and outcome are not identified clearly, we will most likely be unhappy with the outcome.

Too often, churches experience "missional drift" or ambiguity. Here's what we mean by missional drift: It's not unusual, when an activity or event has been occurring for more than two years, the original purpose of the activity or event is no longer the purpose. For example, a church I (Kay) was working with made and sold hundreds of pies every July. The pie sale became the focus of the church for months and the "pie ladies" become a center of control in the church. Resources of time, space, and money became entangled in the pie sale. When asked the purpose of the pie sale, I received multiple answers from the various pie ladies. The pie ladies were not of the same mind. The pie sale had experienced missional drift.  After many questions, I finally discovered the origin of the pie sale began many years earlier when a pastor gave each of the ladies ten dollars, asking them to find a way to double the money as a fundraiser for a local food pantry. Over the years, the pie sale became a fundraiser to purchase things for the church. Among other items, these included a vacuum cleaner and freezer to hold the pies. The original purpose of doubling the financial impact for the local pantry was long forgotten, and the annual pie event became a divisive ministry within the church.

In other churches, it might be the vacation bible school, which was once meant to be an evangelism event to reach new children in the neighborhood. In time, however, VBS became a place for children from churches all over the town to have free babysitting for a week. When ministry team responsible for VBS did not continue to clearly identify the purpose of the event nor the intended outcome, VBS no longer served the intended original purpose.

Once a clearly defined purpose and intended outcome are identified, the next layer of accountability for ministry teams is evaluation. The event is planned around the purpose and outcome. Most often the outcome is tied to the accomplishment of a larger church goal. We often skip this crucial last step in an event, meant to determine if the purpose and intended outcome were met. Instead, we place the event on an annual calendar, never measuring its effectiveness towards the purpose and outcome.

- To hold ministry teams accountable, staff or ministry team leaders will gather the team soon after the event for an evaluation. Ask questions like these:

- Did the activity or event accomplish the intended purpose? If not, why?

- What did we learn?

- Could it be tweaked to serve the purpose if we were to decide to do it again?

In our concert example above, we would ask if 200

unchurched people in the community attended. Did we begin to build relationships? If 200 people attended, but no relationships were built, we only accomplished part of our purpose.

Did the event or activity have the desired outcome? In our concert example, we were looking for two people to become involved in the life of the congregation as a result of attending the concert. If the purpose was met, but the outcome was not achieved, should we hold the event again? Could anything be changed so the outcome would be accomplished? Was the effort invested worth the outcome? Could another event or activity have the same purpose and outcome with less effort/investment or with a better outcome?

This evaluative portion of ministry is extremely important, but sadly we find that many churches struggle to do it. Without these important steps, churches find themselves doing the same event or activity year after year without the desired results. When evaluation is not part of the culture, churches can get stuck doing the same ministries over and over again hoping for a different (more fruitful) outcomes without ever changing. We have somehow convinced ourselves that stopping events or activities means we failed. Sometimes stopping struggling ministries is the most faithful step forward. Not stopping a ministry that has become more about tradition than effectiveness often leads to burnout, frustration, and giving up on our abilities.

## Coaching

*I absolutely believe that people, unless coached,
never reach their maximum capabilities.*

**Bob Nardelli**

Another element in the follow-up strategy is coaching.
The coach is a person outside of the church, ideally the same
person who facilitated the retreat, walking alongside the
pastor and church leaders to provide resources and accountability. This would be referred to as "directive coaching,"
meaning there is an established focus for the coaching, the
church goals. Regular coaching during this process will
help the church stay on track and assist with the harder
parts of implementation, which may include pushback in
certain cases. A person certified by the International Coach
Federation would be ideal. Here is an example of what a
coaching timeline might look like for a church following a
September Strategic Ministry planning retreat:

- October: Phone call with the pastor to review action step
  assignments from the retreat. Discussing communication plans. Addressing any open issues.

- November/December: Online video call with the
  church leaders (staff and ministry team leaders)
  focused on the objectives for each goal, discussing
  budget alignment/approval, and answering questions.

- December: On-site session with pastor individually and
  then meet with the leadership team; ensure everything
  is in place for each church goal; provide encouragement.

- January: Phone call with the pastor. Accountability and support as needed for each church goal.

- February: Online video call with the church leaders. Accountability and support as needed for each church goal

- March: On-site session with pastor, then with the leadership team. Review progress of each goal. Provide encouragement and support.

- April: Phone call with the pastor. Accountability and support as needed for each church goal. Review measurables.

- May: On-line video call with church leaders. Accountability and support as needed for each church goal. Schedule fall strategic planning retreat. Review measurables.

- June: On-site session with pastor individually and then meet with the leadership team. Review measurables. Celebrate progress. Make any adjustments needed based on the church's performance related to each goal.

- July: Phone call with the pastor. Accountability and support as needed for each goal. Discuss plans for setting next year's goals.

- August: Online video call with the church leaders. Accountability and support as needed for each church goal. Discuss plans for setting next year's goals.

- September/October: On-site session with pastor individually and then meet with the leadership team. Review this year's goals and set goals for next year. Conduct the next strategic ministry planning retreat.

This coaching plan is just an example of what coaching

might look like after a strategic ministry planning retreat. Each church situation will look different based on many factors, such as ministry context, and experiences the church and its leaders have had in setting and achieving goals. In this example, we hope you see how the goal setting process will naturally overlap each year. Most churches will still be in the process of working on this year's goals when they begin the process of setting next year's goals.

## Rhythm of Ministry

The last element of follow-up from a strategic ministry planning retreat is one of the most challenging, and one of the most important. We call this the "rhythm" of ministry. Research shows that most of what each of us does each day can be called a habit. We all fall into patterns of life where we do the same things over and over again, often without noticing we are doing them. The same is usually true for a ministry in a church.

Take a look at your last year's church calendar and compare it to the church calendar for this year. They are likely very similar. For a church to achieve new goals each year, logic would say that they must do some things different than they have in the past.

Referring back to *The Four Disciplines of Execution* once more, the authors use the term "whirlwind" to describe existing work and urgent tasks that leaders must do each day, but don't necessarily move the organization forward or accomplish goals. These are not bad activities, just not focused on the future.

Consider your own church and your part in that
ministry. Chances are good that about eighty percent
of your day, week, and month are consumed with these
"whirlwind" type activities. The key is not as much about
changing that percentage as it is on using the remaining
part of your time to focus on achieving goals and
advancing God's Kingdom.

Here are some practical ways to help churches get into a
new rhythm and create a culture of goal achievement:

- Incorporate the church goals into the budget process.
  Most goals will require some type of funding and should
  be reflected in the overall church budget. Too often the
  goal setting process is happening in one room of the
  church, and the budget setting process is happening in
  another room. Be intentional about having both groups
  work together. When there is a new budget request, or
  even requests for funds during the year, ask the question, "How will this support our goal?"

- Add time to your leadership team meetings (Administrative Board, etc.) for goal reviews, updates, and
  support. (See the book, *Mission Possible* by Kay Kotan
  and Blake Bradford for more information on leadership
  team meeting agendas.) A good practice is to open these
  meetings with prayer, spiritual formation, and leadership development; place goal review and other strategic
  conversations in the middle; then end with church business type items such as facilities and finance. We have
  found items not on the agenda will usually be forgotten.
  This is an opportunity for the person who is captaining

each goal to share progress and for the whole leadership team to offer support. For example, let's say it is the July Board/Council meeting and the pastor shares that despite all of the efforts in the first six months, average worship attendance is only up two percent and the goal is a six percent increase for the year. The other leaders need to respond with "What do you need?" and not "Why are you not making your goal?" These are church goals, not individual goals. Church leaders need to be supportive and offer more solutions than criticism.

- Establish an annual "Vision Day" (also commonly referred to as Town Hall Meetings) for the whole congregation. This is best done outside of a worship service. It could be done following your Sunday service if that works best in your church. Vision Days allow the pastor and church leaders to cast visions, provide updates on goal progress, communication goals for the coming year, celebrate all that the church has accomplished in the past year and, in some cases, give an overall state-of-the-church. This session might be led by the pastor and church staff, and should incorporate other ministry leaders (i.e. lay leader, Board/Council Chair) as appropriate. These events are powerful momentum generators for the whole ministry when they are done correctly. They also help build trust and transparency in leadership by the congregation. We recommend holding Vision Days two to four times each year.

The areas we covered in this section: communication, creating objectives, accountability, coaching, and ministry rhythm are all important to ensuring the church achieves the goals it sets and the strategic ministry planning retreat is not just an event, but a catalyst to greater mission and vision fulfillment. We encourage you to write a draft plan to follow up your next retreat. What will follow-up look like for your ministry? What else needs to be included that was not covered in this section? Who can you partner with to review and/or help you create this follow-up plan?

> *Plans fail with no counsel, but with many counselors they succeed.*
>
> **Proverbs 15:22 (CEB)**

# CONCLUSION

## Building a Foundation
## for the Future

*Failure is the most effective
technique to optimize strategic planning,
implementation, and processes.*

**Thomas Edison**

We hope this has proven to be a valuable resource as you prepare, conduct, and follow up a strategic planning retreat. We trust you are reading this conclusion before you start the process as suggested.

After you finish conducting or participating in the strategic planning retreat, we pray you experienced the effectiveness of the time away, the powerfulness of uninterrupted time with the team to dream about God's vision for the church, and the richness of time together building the team. Everything might not have gone as planned. That is perfectly okay.

You will most likely do some things differently next year. You've learned from the experience. You've grown from the experience. Your church is better off for the experience. Each year the process will become easier and more productive as you get used to it and get into the groove. Each year the players will be different, as past team members rolls off and new members join the team.

109

*We believe the essentialness of the annual strategic planning retreat is directly connected to the effectiveness and fruitfulness of the ministry of your church in the upcoming year.*

**Willard & Kotan**

Once a church begins to routinely engage in strategic ministry planning retreats, the leadership will feel off kilter if they do not continue with the strategic ministry planning retreats. Leaders will feel out of balance, ill-prepared, lacking strategy, and working reactively rather than proactively. The work and direction completed at this retreat is priceless and some of the most important if not the most important work of the entire year. This work sets the direction for the life of the congregation for the whole next year. It gives the church a direction, a plan, and a common focus. Without strategic ministry planning, churches find themselves with many silos with their own unique focus and competing for resources.

Remember, while strategic planning is the primary responsibility of the leadership team, the pastor and staff are a huge part, too. The pastor attends and participates in the retreat. The staff receives the goals from the leadership team through the pastor and creates objectives/strategies within their given ministry area so the goals are accomplished. *Everyone* is a part of the plan. *Everyone* is an essential part of the execution of the plan. *Everyone* is rowing in the same direction towards the same destination for a common purpose!

Remember, this was meant to be a resource for a retreat leader to prepare, conduct, and follow up to hold the pastor and leadership team accountable for the following a strategic planning retreat. The heart of the retreat is to walk away with goals which will lead the church into its vision (God's preferred future for the church) in its own unique way of the mission of making disciples. If you walked out of your first strategic ministry planning retreat experience with goals – AMEN! If you walked out of your strategic ministry planning retreat with more than goals on your first retreat – AMEN and AMEN!

Extend yourself some grace and love as you grow into this process each year. At the same time, do NOT give up! The Kingdom rewards are certainly worth the efforts. Be bold and courageous, friends, as you seek to strategically plan for fruitfulness in God's Kingdom.

Remember, growing and vital congregations find strategic ministry planning not as "another thing to do" but rather the foundation built each year to set the most faithful path forward to fulfill the Great Commission. We feel the Great Commission is not merely a nice thing to do or a suggestion. Instead, we feel this is what every church MUST do!

Thank you for allowing us to take you on this journey of strategic ministry planning. We pray this is and will continue to be a blessing to you and your church as you pursue faithfulness in leading your church in both strategic and fruitful ministry planning.

*Planning is bringing the future into the present so that you can do something about it now.*

**Alan Lakein**

# APPENDIX I

## Online Pre-Retreat Survey

**We recommend using a free online survey source such as SurveyMonkey.**

The following is provided as an example survey you can ask the retreat participants to complete. Please adjust it as needed for you and your audience. Remember, people are more likely to complete a short survey (3-10 questions) than they are a long survey.

❑ What is your name and position in ministry?

❑ How did you first hear about this strategic ministry planning retreat?

    a. Leadership team meeting

    b. Other church communication

    c. Personally from a church leader

    d. Your email

    e. Other, please specify.

*Continued on next page*

❑ Which is the best way for us to communicate with you between now and the retreat? (Please rank in order from most preferred to least preferred.)

1. Email

2. Text

3. Phone (please give us the best number to use to reach you)

4. Video Conference

5. Other, please specify.

❑ What questions do you have about the retreat now?

❑ What do you wish most for this ministry to get out of the retreat?

# APPENDIX II

## Self-Study

### Instructions

1. Gather a team to complete this local church self-study. Those leaders who will be participating in the strategic ministry planning retreat should make up the majority of this team. While the pastor can and should be a part of this process, they should not do all the work themselves. Gathering the information is part of the learning process.

2. As each part of the self-study is divided up among the team, give them clear deadlines for completion and where they should go with questions.

3. Once all areas of the self-study are completed and returned, make arrangements to share the entire package with the retreat participants. They should have this complete package delivered to them no later than 30 days prior to the retreat so they will have time to read and process the information.

4. In our experience, most churches can complete the entire self-study in three to four months. This allows for time to pull all of the parts back together and then share the information with the retreat participants.

5. While this self-study may focus a lot on data, statistics, numbers, and information, that should not mean anyone should "turn off God" during the process. We encourage you to make this whole work a prayerful, Spirit-filled process. Each person completing their individual part of the self-study should be encouraged to spend time in God's Word and prayer before, during, and after they complete their assigned section.

## Section One – History

### Read Acts, Chapter 2

Pentecost is often referred to as the "birth of the church." What stands out to you about these verses? What do phrases such as, "They were all together in one place," or "He poured out this Spirit," or "The Lord added daily to the community" mean to your ministry today?

1. Write a brief history of the church/congregation [one-page front and back max]. Be sure to include the origin story of the church. Include those events that contributed to periods of growth or decline in attendance. Write in a factual style, avoiding the temptation to exaggerate information or inject personal commentary. (This should not focus on facilities, but mostly on church ministry.)

2. What are the major conflicts the church has seen in the past? How would you describe the current state of those conflicts? What, if anything, needs to be done now to resolve any current church conflicts?

3. List dates and provide descriptions for any building construction, major renovations, land acquisitions, or leasing of facilities. List the amount of acreage the church owns, leases, or rents and the square footage of all buildings, including homes/parsonage.

4. List any formal ties or major connections to other congregations, organizations, or associations. State how the congregation views and interacts with these groups.

5. Provide a listing of all full and part-time paid program staff positions, including pastors, for the last twenty years. Give the dates of tenure and state the reason why they left, if permissible.

6. Provide a list of all people who currently oversee specific areas of ministry. These may be paid positions; in many churches they will be unpaid positions. Create an organizational chart which reflects your current structure. Be sure all committees, ministries, teams, groups, and anything else pertinent to this process are included.

## Section Two – Statistics

**Read Matthew 14:13-21, Mark 8:1-10, and Numbers 1:2**

People matter to God. We count people because people count. The Bible is full of statistics and numbers. We tend to see them only as numbers and too many churches and Christians have developed a fear of data. Every number is important to God because they represent people. Facts are our friends. How do you feel about numbers and statistics? Pray to God now to open you up to see what the Lord sees. (The first two areas of the following are specifically for United Methodist Churches. If your church is not UMC, you will need to find other resources to gather this information. But please do not skip this section.)

7. Go to the website www.umdata.org. Click on the button that says, "STATS." Click on the "Charges/Churches" option listed on the left. Select your Jurisdiction, select your Conference, and select your District. Locate the name of your church on the list and click on it. At the bottom of the Charts section on the left side of the page is a button which says, "Healthy Church Initiative Download." Click on that button and an Excel workbook will download which you can name and save to your computer. This file will give you information your church has submitted for year-end statistics over the last 20 or more years.

8. Using this information, create two charts based on the yearly statistics. Go back as far as possible and be sure to include last year, even if it has not been added to this file. One chart should show average attendance and membership for each year. The second chart should include total professions of faith, removed by death, and total baptisms.

9. Estimate the median age of people participating in regularly scheduled worship services in your church. Explain how you came up with this number.

10. State the percentage of people who attend your worship services who also attend some form of Christian community (Sunday school, small group meetings, Celebrate Recovery, other support groups, etc.). Count each individual only once.

11. Prepare a list of the number of current members of your church, or regular attenders, who got involved in your church:

    a.  Before 1980
    b.  From 1980 to 1989
    c.  From 1990 to 1999
    d.  From 2000 to 2009
    e.  From 2010 to 2019
    f.  From 2020 to present.

12. Without listing names, state the amount given by each of the top ten contributors on record in the last fiscal year. Total these amounts and state the percentage of giving this represents in relation to the total of all contributions.

13. State the same information as above for the next ten contributors on record.

14. State the total number of contributors to the church during the last fiscal year and the average amount given per contributor during that time.

15. What percentage of the annual budget is going to pay off debt (mortgage payment, etc.)?

## Section Three – Community Study

*For where two or three are gathered in my name, I'm there with them.*

**Jesus, Matthew 18:20 (NIV)**

16. Write a brief overview of the area and community in which the church building is located and where you primarily serve. (Typically, this is one to two miles around the main church building.)

17. Community Leader Interviews. Speak with at least five different key leaders in your community. Examples include but are not limited to: police chief, fire chief, school principle, business leader, social worker, school counselor, mayor or other government official, chamber of commerce president. The objective here is to gain a new perspective on your mission field. Honor the time of the person you are speaking with by limiting your conversation to 30 minutes or less. Share the following with the person you are interviewing, in your own words: "Our church is talking to community leaders such as yourself to better understand the community we feel God has called us to serve. Thank you for taking the time to speak with me today. I just have a few questions to ask. I'm going to take notes as we talk so we can compile all of our interviews."

a. Based on your position in our community, what do you see at the top two or three needs of our community?

b. From your unique perspective, what do you know about our community that others might not know?

c. What would you like to see a local church do to improve our community?

d. What would you like to share with our church about this community?

Thank them again for their time. Once all of the interviews have been completed, compile the notes together by question. Identify any trends you see. Highlight comments to support those trends.

## Section Four – Demographics

You will need to have access to and have a basic understanding of the MissionInsite online system to complete this section of the self-study. All United Methodist churches have access to this system through their conference. If you are not part of The United Methodist Church, you can still access this data through MissionInsite, you will just need to pay the fee to join first.

18. Log into MissionInsite and go to the "People Plot" section. If you have not already done so, watch the video on how to upload people in your church into the MissionInsite system, and upload the Excel sheet as instructed.

a. Choose your church from the dropdown list on the next page "Let's Decide Which Congregants You Want to Plot" and click "Next."

b. On the "Now, Let's Decide How the Plots Should be Color - Coded" page, leave the "Legend By..." section on "None," check the box "Show Labels," and then click "Next."

c. On the "Review and Summary" page, click on "Finish."

d. Zoom-in on the map on the next page until you see your church building and the names of people in your congregation.

e. On the left side of the page you should see an icon of a pen called, "Draw New Shape and Query" when you click on it, you will be able to create a shape around where the majority of your congregation lives.

## IMPORTANT NOTES:

1) Try to keep your church in the approximate center of the shape.

2) Try to include most, but not all of your congregation in the shape, it is very common for some people to drive further than others to attend church, keep your focus close to the building while working to include at least 80 percent of your worshiping congregation.

3) Do not forget to close the shape by connecting the last point with the first point.

- Once you have your shape, click on the "demographics" button at the bottom of the page. On the far right you will now see a "Demographics" section, under "Predefined" click on the dropdown next to "Select a predefined report." Be sure to click on your shape so you are not running reports for a larger area. You will know because your shape will be shown on the first page of the report.

19. Run the following reports: ExecutiveInsite, ComparativeInsite, MinistryInsite Priorities, and ReligiousInsite Priorities.

a. Print a copy of each report (double-sided and in color if possible). Save a copy of each report in case you need to print them again.

b. As you are reviewing all of the information contained within these reports, be sure to answer these questions concerning your mission field (the area of the shape you created):

- What is the total population? Has that population been growing, declining, or staying flat over the past years? How does your church's worship attendance trend compare to the population trend?

- What are the racial-ethnic trends? Does your congregation represent your mission field racially?

- What is the average age of your mission field? How does that compare to your church?

- What is the average household income?

- What percentage of households with children are single parent? How does your church minister with single parents?

- What are the percentages of white collar to blue collar? How does that compare to your church?

- What are the percentages of each generation in your mission field? How does that compare to your congregation?

- What percentage of people in your mission field are NOT active in a religious congregation or community? How is your church reaching out to these people?

- What "Mosaic Segments" in your mission field is the church reaching now? Which ones does the church need to focus on reaching?

- What percentage of the church's potential giving is the church currently receiving?

20. What are the top three to five things you learned from these reports which should influence how the church does ministry in the next few years?

## Section Five – Documents

*The Lord replied, "Who are the faithful and wise managers whom the master will put in charge of his household servants, to give them their food at the proper time? Happy are the servants whom the master finds fulfilling their responsibilities when he comes. I assure you that the master will put them in charge of all his possessions."*

**Jesus, Luke 12:42-44 (NIV)**

21. Gather the following documents or their equivalents:

a. Last two years charge conference reports. Focusing on what the church has accomplished in ministry during the past two years.

124

b. Last two annual budgets and full financial statements, for the past two fiscal years, as well as the most recent financial report for this current year. Be sure to include budget versus actual and balance sheets.

c. Sample bulletins and newsletters, for several seasons if possible. Gather at least six of each.

d. Any policy statements or policy manuals.

e. Other printed documents or printouts of online information you feel would be helpful in providing insight into the church.

Ask at least three people to review this collection of church documents. They do not need to be financial experts or church leaders. In fact, it might be better for them to be representative of the church's "average" member or attender. In reviewing all these documents, 1) What words or phrases seem to come up the most often? 2) What do they indicate is most important to the church? 3) What surprises you?

## Section Six – Discipleship

> *Therefore, go and make disciples of all nations, baptizing them in the name of the Father and of the Son and of the Holy Spirit, teaching them to obey everything that I've commanded you. Look, I myself will be with you every day until the end of this present age.*

**Jesus, Matthew 28:19-20**

22. What is the church's intentional process for growing disciples?

23. What indicators have you seen that this discipleship process is producing fruit?

24. How does a new to this church person get engaged with the discipleship process?

25. What are the church's next steps in the area of discipleship?

## Section Seven – Questionnaire

A best practice is to assemble a team of four people to complete the following questionnaire together. This team would have a representative from trustees, finance, hospitality, and children's ministry. The intention is for them to complete the entire document together and to then present their findings with any supporting information back to the appropriate person coordinating the overall self-study.

26. How many parking spaces are available for each worship service? Does the church have enough off-street parking spaces to accommodate at least 80 percent of your average worship attendance? How many parking spaces have signs designating them as handicap, first-time guest, new/expecting mother, or other designation?

27. How many adult Sunday school classes does the church currently have in place? Small groups? Support or recovery groups? Are any of these larger than 15 people? When was the last time the church started a new adult Sunday school class or small group?

28. What is the total capacity of the sanctuary or main worship space? (If using pews, measure the actual pew length and divide by 24 inches.) What is 80 percent of total capacity? How does that compare to the church's current average worship attendance?

29. What is the total capacity of the nursery? How often is the nursery at capacity during a worship service? Are infants and toddlers separated? Is nursery available for all church events? Are you using Safe Sanctuary guidelines? Is the church compliant to all Safe Sanctuary guidelines, including having uncovered glass windows in all doors? How often are toys cleaned? How often are toys replaced? What is the church's plan for children in case of an emergency? What type of check-in system is the church using? What is the procedure for checking a child into the ministry area for the first time? How are children with food allergies or other medical issues kept safe? Are the public schools in the area growing, stable, or declining? (Have data to support your conclusion.) How many children, on average, are in each ministry room each week? What is the church's children-to-adults ratio overall? How are children in the church being grown as a disciple?

30. What days of the week and what hours does the church offer worship each week? How were those days and times chosen? When was the last time the church changed the number of worship services and/or the worship times? How would you describe the types of service and music being offered at each worship? (Using words and phrases a non-church going person would understand. The words "traditional" and "contemporary" do not mean anything to people outside the church.)

31. Is there an adequate/attractive sign perpendicular to the street with worship times clearly visible (can you read them from a car driving the speed limit) to inform new guests? Is there signage from the parking area(s) directing new guests to the correct entrance door? Are there clear/attractive signs inside the building to help new guests find their way? (The most important areas are the nursery, rest rooms, and worship space.)

32. How many first-time guest families does the church average each week? (A good rule is the total number of "new here," first-time guests per year should be equal to or higher than the average number attending worship.) What is the connections system to know who is a first-time guest each week? What do first-time guest receive from the church on that initial visit? How and when are those new guests contacted?

33. What is the church's process for becoming a member? How are people trained and equipped to serve in ministry at the church? How many people are involved in serving at the church each week? What percentage is that to the average in worship? How many people served for the first time last year?

34. What is the church's process for becoming a ministry leader? How are people trained and equipped to lead a ministry? What is the church's plan to grow both its current leaders and new leaders?

## Section Eight – Leadership Questions

*Do nothing out of selfish ambition or vain conceit, but in humility, consider others better than yourselves. Each of you should look not only to your own interests, but also to the interests of others.*

**Apostle Paul, Philippians 2:3-4 (NIV)**

Once you have completed all the previous questions and gathered all of the necessary documents and information, pull it together in a binder or some other form so you can share copies with each person who will be participating in the strategic ministry planning retreat and the facilitator. Give everyone some time to review and process the information, at least 30 days. Ask them to pray for God's Spirit to give them discernment and wisdom as they study the package of information. After a careful review of the total self-study package, each retreat participant needs to answer the following questions:

- What are the top five strengths of this congregation in priority order?

- What are the two or three most significant challenges/areas of weakness we need to address in the next 12-18 months?

- What do we need to change soon to best reach our mission field and make disciples of Jesus?

- What should NOT change?

- Do you want to see this congregation grow significantly in the next five years? Why or why not?

- Are you willing to make the difficult decisions required for change and growth? Are you willing to set aside personal preferences to do what the church leaders feel is best for God's Kingdom?

# APPENDIX III

## Core Values Survey Example

**Instructions: Place an "X" in the appropriate column**

- Choose five (5) values you feel our ministry demonstrates consistently and guide all that we do.
- Choose three (3) values you feel our ministry demonstrates, but not consistently.
- Choose two (2) values you feel are not in place currently in our ministry, but should be for us to become the church God is calling us to be.

| | Value | Consistent | Inconsistent | Aspirational |
|---|---|---|---|---|
| 1 | Fellowship - enjoying time with each other | | | |
| 2 | Prayer - communicating with God | | | |
| 3 | Excellence - doing our very best in all we do | | | |
| 4 | Servanthood - putting others first | | | |
| 5 | Worship - gathering to praise God | | | |
| 6 | Preaching - sharing God's Word | | | |

| | | | | |
|---|---|---|---|---|
| 7 | Apply Scripture - putting God's Word into action | | | |
| 8 | Innovation - new ways to be more effective | | | |
| 9 | Tradition - honoring the past | | | |
| 10 | Compassion - caring for the well-being of others | | | |
| 11 | Leadership - growing the ability to influence | | | |
| 12 | Outreach - caring for those around us | | | |
| 13 | Missions - caring for those around the world | | | |
| 14 | Creativity - artistic ways to do ministry | | | |
| 15 | Discipleship - creating followers of Jesus | | | |
| 16 | Evangelism - telling others about Jesus | | | |
| 17 | Generosity - offering our money to God | | | |
| 18 | Encouragement - offering hope and support | | | |
| 19 | Diversity - embracing differences among us | | | |
| 20 | Mobilized - equipping everyone to help | | | |
| 21 | Bible - know and remember biblical truths | | | |
| 22 | Families - engaging multiple generations | | | |

| | | | | |
|---|---|---|---|---|
| 23 | Integrity - doing what we say we will do | | | |
| 24 | Unchurched - attracting those who do not attend church | | | |
| 25 | Intentionality - planning for what we must do | | | |
| 26 | Obedience - following God and leaders | | | |
| 27 | Christian Groups - gathering to grow in faith | | | |
| 28 | Christ-Centered - ensuring all we do reflects Jesus | | | |
| 29 | Children & Youth - helping kids grow in faith | | | |
| 30 | Cooperation - working together to serve Jesus | | | |
| 31 | Risk-Taking - willing to try new things | | | |
| 32 | Relevance - understandable and applicable today | | | |
| 33 | Accountability - holding people responsible | | | |
| 34 | Growth - expand our reach and impact | | | |
| 35 | Authenticity - being ourselves always | | | |
| 36 | Fruitfulness - focus on results for God's Kingdom | | | |
| 37 | Joy - fun, laughter, and amusement | | | |
| 38 | Open-minded - able to consider other ideas and perspectives | | | |

# Recent Titles

## from Market Square Books

marketsquarebooks.com

### From Heaven To Earth

Wil Cantrell & Paul Seay

### Tidings of Comfort and Joy

Charles W. Maynard

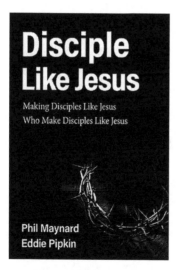

### Disciple Like Jesus

Making Disciples Like Jesus Who Make Disciples Like Jesus

Phil Maynard & Eddie Pipkin

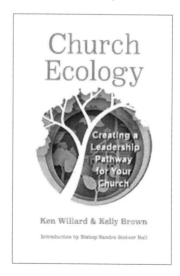

### Church Ecology

Ken Willard & Kelly Brown

# Other Books
## from Market Square

marketsquarebooks.com

**Wesleyan Grace Theology**

Dr. Donald Haynes

**Where Do We Go From Here?**

24 United Methodist Writers

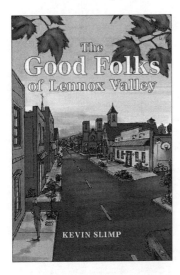

**The Good Folks of Lennox Valley**

Kevin Slimp

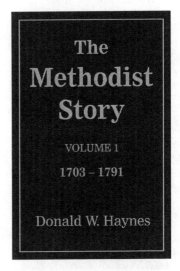

**The Methodist Story Volume I ▪ 1703-1791**

Dr. Donald Haynes

# Grow Your Faith

## with these books from Market Square

marketsquarebooks.com

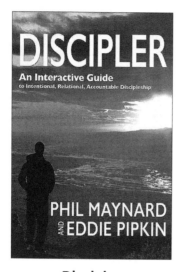

**Discipler**

Phil Maynard & Eddie Pipkin

**Hear It, See It, Risk It**

Steve Cordle

**A Christian Teenager's**
**Guide to Surviving High School**

Ashley Conner

**Understanding Your Call**
**11 Biblical Figures Understand**
**Their Calls from God**

by 10 United Methodist Leaders

# Grow Your Church

## with these books from Market Square

marketsquarebooks.com

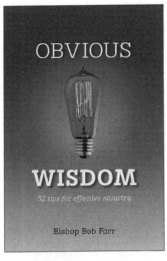

**Obvious Wisdom**

Bishop Bob Farr

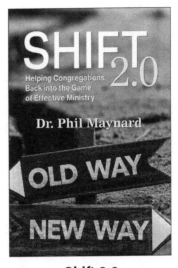

**Shift 2.0**

Phil Maynard

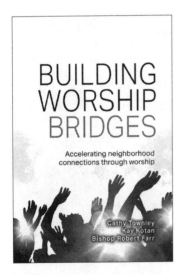

**Building Worship Bridges**

Cathy Townley

**Get Out of That Box!**

Anne Bosarge

# Latest Titles

## from Market Square Books

marketsquarebooks.com

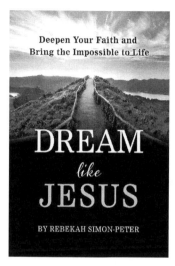

**Dream Like Jesus**
**Bring the Impossible to Life**
Rebekah Simon-Peter

**From Franchise**
**To Local Dive**
Jason Moore & Rosario Picardo

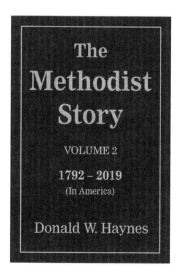

**The Methodist Story**
**Volume 2 ▪ 1792-2019**
Dr. Donald W. Haynes

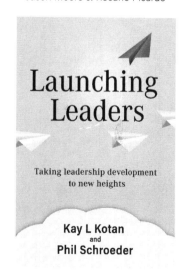

**Launching Leaders**
**Leadership Development**
Kay Kotan and Phil Schroeder